FastAPI
Modern Python Web Development

Bill Lubanovic

Beijing · Boston · Farnham · Sebastopol · Tokyo

FastAPI

by Bill Lubanovic

Published by O'Reilly Media, Inc., 1005 Gravenstein Highway North, Sebastopol, CA 95472.

O'Reilly books may be purchased for educational, business, or sales promotional use. Online editions are also available for most titles (*https://oreilly.com*). For more information, contact our corporate/institutional sales department: 800-998-9938 or *corporate@oreilly.com*.

Acquisitions Editor: Amanda Quinn
Development Editor: Corbin Collins
Production Editor: Kristen Brown
Copyeditor: Sharon Wilkey
Proofreader: Liz Wheeler

Indexer: BIM Creatives, LLC
Interior Designer: David Futato
Cover Designer: Karen Montgomery
Illustrator: Kate Dullea

November 2023:   First Edition

Revision History for the First Edition

2023-11-06:   First Release

See *http://oreilly.com/catalog/errata.csp?isbn=9781098135508* for release details.

978-1-098-13550-8

[LSI]

To the loving memory of my wife, Mary, my parents, Bill and Tillie, and my friend, Rich.
I miss you.

Table of Contents

Part I.   What's New?

Part II.   A FastAPI Tour

Part IV.   A Gallery

Preface

This is a pragmatic introduction to FastAPI—a modern Python web framework. It's also a story of how, now and then, the bright and shiny objects that we stumble across can turn out to be very useful. A silver bullet is nice to have when you encounter a werewolf. (And you will encounter werewolves later in this book.)

I started programming scientific applications in the mid-1970s. And after I first met Unix and C on a PDP-11 in 1977, I had a feeling that this Unix thing might catch on.

In the '80s and early '90s, the internet was still noncommercial, but already a good source for free software and technical info. And when a web browser called Mosaic was distributed on the baby open internet in 1993, I had a feeling that this web thing might catch on.

When I started my own web development company a few years later, my tools were the usual suspects at the time: PHP, HTML, and Perl. On a contract job a few years later, I finally experimented with Python and was surprised at how quickly I was able to access, manipulate, and display data. In my spare time over two weeks, I was able to replicate most of a C application that had taken four developers a year to write. Now I had a feeling that this Python thing might catch on.

After that, most of my work involved Python and its web frameworks, mostly Flask and Django. I particularly liked the simplicity of Flask and preferred it for many jobs. But just a few years ago, I spied something glinting in the underbrush: a new Python web framework called FastAPI, written by Sebastián Ramírez.

As I read his (excellent) documentation (*https://fastapi.tiangolo.com*), I was impressed by the design and thought that had gone into it. In particular, his history (*https://oreil.ly/Ds-xM*) page showed how much care he had taken evaluating alternatives. This was not an ego project or a fun experiment, but a serious framework for real-world development. Now I had a feeling that this FastAPI thing might catch on.

I wrote a biomedical API site with FastAPI, and it went so well that a team of us rewrote our old core API with FastAPI in the next year. This is still in production and has held up well. Our group learned the basics that you'll read in this book, and all felt that we were writing better code, faster, with fewer bugs. And by the way, some of us had not written in Python before, and only I had used FastAPI.

So when I had an opportunity to suggest a follow-up to my *Introducing Python* book to O'Reilly, FastAPI was at the top of my list. In my opinion, FastAPI will have at least the impact that Flask and Django have had, and maybe more.

As I've mentioned, the FastAPI website itself provides world-class documentation, including many details on the usual web topics: databases, authentication, deployment, and so on. So why write a book?

This book isn't meant to be exhaustive because, well, that's exhausting. It *is* meant to be useful—to help you quickly pick up the main ideas of FastAPI and apply them. I will point out various techniques that required some sleuthing and offer advice on day-to-day best practices.

I start each chapter with a Preview of what's coming. Next, I try not to forget what I just promised, offering details and random asides. Finally, there's a brief digestible Review.

As the saying goes, "These are the opinions on which my facts are based." Your experience will be unique, but I hope that you will find enough of value here to become a more productive web developer.

Conventions Used in This Book

The following typographical conventions are used in this book:

Italic
: Indicates new terms, URLs, email addresses, filenames, and file extensions.

`Constant width`
: Used for program listings, as well as within paragraphs to refer to program elements such as variable or function names, databases, data types, environment variables, statements, and keywords.

`Constant width bold`
: Shows commands or other text that should be typed literally by the user.

`Constant width italic`
: Shows text that should be replaced with user-supplied values or by values determined by context.

This element signifies a tip or suggestion.

 This element signifies a general note.

Using Code Examples

Supplemental material (code examples, exercises, etc.) is available for download at *https://github.com/madscheme/fastapi*.

If you have a technical question or a problem using the code examples, please send email to *support@oreilly.com*.

This book is here to help you get your job done. In general, if example code is offered with this book, you may use it in your programs and documentation. You do not need to contact us for permission unless you're reproducing a significant portion of the code. For example, writing a program that uses several chunks of code from this book does not require permission. Selling or distributing examples from O'Reilly books does require permission. Answering a question by citing this book and quoting example code does not require permission. Incorporating a significant amount of example code from this book into your product's documentation does require permission.

We appreciate, but generally do not require, attribution. An attribution usually includes the title, author, publisher, and ISBN. For example: "*FastAPI* by Bill Lubanovic (O'Reilly). Copyright 2024 Bill Lubanovic, 978-1-098-13550-8."

If you feel your use of code examples falls outside fair use or the permission given above, feel free to contact us at *permissions@oreilly.com*.

O'Reilly Online Learning

 For more than 40 years, *O'Reilly Media* has provided technology and business training, knowledge, and insight to help companies succeed.

Our unique network of experts and innovators share their knowledge and expertise through books, articles, and our online learning platform. O'Reilly's online learning platform gives you on-demand access to live training courses, in-depth learning paths, interactive coding environments, and a vast collection of text and video from O'Reilly and 200+ other publishers. For more information, visit *https://oreilly.com*.

How to Contact Us

Please address comments and questions concerning this book to the publisher:

> O'Reilly Media, Inc.
> 1005 Gravenstein Highway North
> Sebastopol, CA 95472
> 800-889-8969 (in the United States or Canada)
> 707-829-7019 (international or local)
> 707-829-0104 (fax)
> *support@oreilly.com*
> *https://www.oreilly.com/about/contact.html*

We have a web page for this book, where we list errata, examples, and any additional information. You can access this page at *https://oreil.ly/FastAPI*.

For news and information about our books and courses, visit *https://oreilly.com*.

Find us on LinkedIn: *https://linkedin.com/company/oreilly-media*.

Follow us on Twitter: *https://twitter.com/oreillymedia*.

Watch us on YouTube: *https://youtube.com/oreillymedia*.

Acknowledgments

Thanks to many people, at many places, from whom I've learned so much:

- Serra High School
- The University of Pittsburgh
- The Chronobiology Laboratories, University of Minnesota
- Intran
- Crosfield-Dicomed
- Northwest Airlines
- Tela
- WAM!NET
- Mad Scheme
- SSESCO
- Intradyn
- Keep
- Thomson Reuters
- Cray
- Penguin Computing
- Internet Archive
- CrowdStrike
- Flywheel

## PART I

What's New?

The world has benefited greatly from the invention of the World Wide Web by Sir Tim Berners-Lee,[1] and the Python programming language by Guido van Rossum.

The only tiny problem is that a nameless computer book publisher often puts spiders and snakes on its relevant web and Python covers. If only the web had been named the World Wide *Woof* (cross-threads in weaving, also called *weft*), and Python were *Pooch*, this book might have had a cover like Figure I-1.

Figure I-1. FastAPI: Modern Pooch Woof Development

---

1 I actually shook his hand once. I didn't wash mine for a month, but I'll bet he did right away.

But I digress.[2] This book is about the following:

The web
 An especially productive technology, how it has changed, and how to develop software for it now

Python
 An especially productive web development language

FastAPI
 An especially productive Python web framework

The two chapters in this first part discuss emerging topics in the web and in Python: services and APIs; concurrency; layered architectures; and big, big data.

Part II is a high-level tour of FastAPI, a fresh Python web framework that has good answers to the questions posed in Part I.

Part III rummages deeper through the FastAPI toolbox, including tips learned during production development.

Finally, Part IV provides a gallery of FastAPI web examples. They use a common data source—imaginary creatures—that may be a little more interesting and cohesive than the usual random expositions. These should give you a starting point for particular applications.

---

2 Not for the last time.

## CHAPTER 1

The Modern Web

The Web as I envisaged it, we have not seen it yet. The future is still so much bigger than the past.

—Tim Berners-Lee

Preview

Once upon a time, the web was small and simple. Developers had such fun throwing PHP, HTML, and MySQL calls into single files and proudly telling everyone to check out their website. But the web grew over time to zillions, nay, squillions of pages— and the early playground became a metaverse of theme parks.

In this chapter, I'll point out some areas that have become ever more relevant to the modern web:

- Services and APIs
- Concurrency
- Layers
- Data

The next chapter will show what Python offers in these areas. After that, we'll dive into the FastAPI web framework and see what it has to offer.

Services and APIs

The web is a great connecting fabric. Although much activity still occurs on the *content* side—HTML, JavaScript, images, and so on—there's an increasing emphasis on the application programming interfaces (APIs) that connect things.

Commonly, a web *service* handles low-level database access and middle-level business logic (often lumped together as a *backend*), while JavaScript or mobile apps provide a rich top-level *frontend* (interactive user interface). These fore and aft worlds have become more complex and divergent, usually requiring developers to specialize in one or the other. It's harder to be a *full stack* developer than it used to be.[1]

These two worlds talk to each other using APIs. In the modern web, API design is as important as the design of websites themselves. An API is a contract, similar to a database schema. Defining and modifying APIs is now a major job.

Kinds of APIs

Each API defines the following:

Protocol
    The control structure

Format
    The content structure

Multiple API methods have developed as technology has evolved from isolated machines, to multitasking systems, to networked servers. You'll probably run across one or more of these at some point, so the following is a brief summary before getting to *HTTP* and its friends, which are featured in this book:

- Before networking, an API usually meant a very close connection, like a function call to a *library* in the same language as your application—say, calculating a square root in a math library.

- *Remote procedure calls (RPCs)* were invented to call functions in other processes, on the same machine or others, as though they were in the calling application. A popular current example is gRPC (*https://grpc.io*).

- *Messaging* sends small chunks of data in pipelines among processes. Messages may be verb-like commands or may just indicate noun-like *events* of interest. Current popular messaging solutions, which vary broadly from toolkits to full servers, include Apache Kafka (*https://kafka.apache.org*), RabbitMQ (*https://*

---

1 I gave up trying a few years ago.

www.rabbitmq.com), NATS (*https://nats.io*), and ZeroMQ (*https://zeromq.org*). Communication can follow different patterns:

Request-response
> One: one, like a web browser calling a web server.

Publish-subscribe, or pub-sub
> A *publisher* emits messages, and *subscribers* act on each according to some data in the message, like a subject.

Queues
> Like pub-sub, but only one of a pool of subscribers grabs the message and acts on it.

Any of these may be used alongside a web service—for example, performing a slow backend task like sending an email or creating a thumbnail image.

HTTP

Berners-Lee proposed three components for his World Wide Web:

HTML
> A language for displaying data

HTTP
> A client-server protocol

URLs
> An addressing scheme for web resources

Although these seem obvious in retrospect, they turned out to be a ridiculously useful combination. As the web evolved, people experimented, and some ideas, like the IMG tag, survived the Darwinian struggle. And as needs became clearer, people got serious about defining standards.

REST(ful)

One chapter in Roy Fielding's Ph.D. thesis (*https://oreil.ly/TwGmX*) defined *Representational State Transfer (REST)*—an *architectural style* for HTTP use.[2] Although often referenced, it's been largely misunderstood (*https://oreil.ly/bsSry*).

---

2 *Style* means a higher-level pattern, like *client-server*, rather than a specific design.

A roughly shared adaptation has evolved and dominates the modern web. It's called *RESTful*, with these characteristics:

- Uses HTTP and client-server protocol
- Stateless (each connection is independent)
- Cacheable
- Resource-based

A *resource* is data that you can distinguish and perform operations on. A web service provides an *endpoint*—a distinct URL and HTTP *verb* (action)—for each feature that it wants to expose. An endpoint is also called a *route*, because it routes the URL to a function.

Database users are familiar with the *CRUD* acronym of procedures: create, read, update, delete. The HTTP verbs are pretty CRUDdy:

POST
    Create (write)

PUT
    Modify completely (replace)

PATCH
    Modify partially (update)

GET
    Um, get (read, retrieve)

DELETE
    Uh, delete

A client sends a *request* to a RESTful endpoint with data in one of the following areas of an HTTP message:

- Headers
- The URL string
- Query parameters
- Body values

In turn, an HTTP *response* returns these:

- An integer *status code* (*https://oreil.ly/oBena*) indicating the following:

    100s
        Info, keep going

200s
> Success

300s
> Redirection

400s
> Client error

500s
> Server error

- Various headers
- A body, which may be empty, single, or *chunked* (in successive pieces)

At least one status code is an Easter egg: 418 (I'm a teapot (*https://www.google.com/teapot*)) is supposed to be returned by a web-connected teapot, if asked to brew coffee.

You'll find many websites and books on RESTful API design, all with useful rules of thumb. This book will dole some out on the way.

JSON and API Data Formats

Frontend applications can exchange plain ASCII text with backend web services, but how can you express data structures like lists of things?

Just about when we really started to need it, along came *JavaScript Object Notation (JSON)*—another simple idea that solves an important problem and seems obvious with hindsight. Although the *J* stands for *JavaScript*, the syntax looks a lot like Python too.

JSON has largely replaced older attempts like XML and SOAP. In the rest of this book, you'll see that JSON is the default web service input and output format.

JSON:API

The combination of RESTful design and JSON data formats is common now. But some wiggle room still remains for ambiguity and nerd tussles. The recent JSON:API (*https://jsonapi.org*) proposal aims to tighten specs a bit. This book will use the loose RESTful approach, but JSON:API or something similarly rigorous may be useful if you have significant tussles.

GraphQL

RESTful interfaces can be cumbersome for some purposes. Facebook (now Meta) designed Graph Query Language (*GraphQL*) (*https://graphql.org*) to specify more flexible service queries. I won't go into GraphQL in this book, but you may want to look into it if you find RESTful design inadequate for your application.

Concurrency

Besides the growth of service orientation, the rapid expansion of the number of connections to web services requires ever better efficiency and scale.

We want to reduce the following:

Latency
　　The up-front wait time

Throughput
　　The number of bytes per second between the service and its callers

In the old web days,[3] people dreamed of supporting hundreds of simultaneous connections, then fretted about the "10K problem," and now assume millions at a time.

The term *concurrency* doesn't mean full parallelism. Multiple processing isn't occurring in the same nanosecond, in a single CPU. Instead, concurrency mostly avoids *busy waiting* (idling the CPU until a response is delivered). CPUs are zippy, but networks and disks are thousands to millions of times slower. So, whenever we talk to a network or disk, we don't want to just sit there with a blank stare until it responds.

Normal Python execution is *synchronous*: one thing at a time, in the order specified by the code. Sometimes we want to be *asynchronous*: do a little of one thing, then a little of another thing, back to the first thing, and so on. If all our code uses the CPU to calculate things (*CPU bound*), there's really no spare time to be asynchronous. But if we perform something that makes the CPU wait for an external thing to complete (I/O bound), we can be asynchronous.

Asynchronous systems provide an *event loop*: requests for slow operations are sent and noted, but we don't hold up the CPU waiting for their responses. Instead, some

---

3 Around when caveman played hacky sack with giant ground sloths.

immediate processing is done on each pass through the loop, and any responses that came in during that time are handled in the next pass.

The effects can be dramatic. Later in this book, you'll see how FastAPI's support of asynchronous processing makes it much faster than typical web frameworks.

Asynchronous processing isn't magic. You still have to be careful to avoid doing too much CPU-intensive work during the event loop, because that will slow down everything. Later in this book, you'll see the uses of Python's `async` and `await` keywords, and how FastAPI lets you mix both synchronous and asynchronous processing.

Layers

Shrek fans may remember he noted his layers of personality, to which Donkey replied, "Like an onion?"

Well, if ogres and tearful vegetables can have layers, then so can software. To manage size and complexity, many applications have long used a so-called *three-tier model*.[4] This isn't terribly new. Terms differ,[5] but for this book I'm using the following simple separation of terms (see Figure 1-1):

Web
    Input/output layer over HTTP, which assembles client requests, calls the Service Layer, and returns responses

Service
    The business logic, which calls the Data layer when needed

Data
    Access to data stores and other services

Model
    Data definitions shared by all layers

---

4 Choose your own dialect: tier/layer, tomato/tomahto/arigato.

5 You'll often see the term *Model-View-Controller (MVC)* and variations. Commonly accompanied by religious wars, toward which I'm agnostic.

Web client
  Web browser or other HTTP client-side software

Database
  The data store, often an SQL or NoSQL server

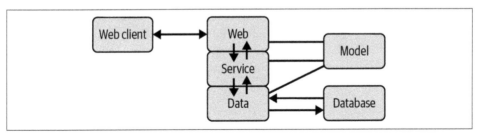

Figure 1-1. Vertical layers

These components will help you scale your site without having to start from scratch. They're not laws of quantum mechanics, so consider them guidelines for this book's exposition.

The layers talk to one another via APIs. These can be simple function calls to separate Python modules, but could access external code via any method. As I showed earlier, this could include RPCs, messages, and so on. In this book, I'm assuming a single web server, with Python code importing other Python modules. The separation and information hiding is handled by the modules.

The *Web layer* is the one that users see, via *client* applications and APIs. We're usually talking about a RESTful web interface, with URLs, and JSON-encoded requests and responses. But alternative text (or command-line interface, CLI) clients also could be built alongside the Web layer. Python Web code may import Service-layer modules but should not import Data modules.

The *Service layer* contains the actual details of whatever this website provides. This layer essentially looks like a *library*. It imports Data modules to access databases and external services but should not know the details.

The *Data layer* provides the Service layer access to data, through files or client calls to other services. Alternative Data layers may also exist, communicating with a single Service layer.

The *Model box* isn't an actual layer but a source of data definitions shared by the layers. This isn't needed if you're passing built-in Python data structures among them. As you will see, FastAPI's inclusion of Pydantic enables the definition of data structures with many useful features.

Why make these divisions? Among many reasons, each layer can be:

- Written by specialists.
- Tested in isolation.
- Replaced or supplemented: you might add a second Web layer, using a different API such as gRPC, alongside a web one.

Follow one rule from *Ghostbusters*: Don't cross the streams. That is, don't let web details leak out of the Web layer, or database details out of the Data layer.

You can visualize *layers* as a vertical stack, like a cake in the Great British Bake Off.[6]

Here are some reasons for separation of the layers:

- If you don't separate the layers, expect a hallowed web meme: *Now you have two problems.*
- Once the layers are mixed, later separation will be *very* difficult.
- You'll need to know two or more specialties to understand and write tests if code logic gets muddled.

By the way, even though I call them *layers*, you don't need to assume that one layer is "above" or "below" another, and that commands flow with gravity. Vertical chauvinism! You could also view layers as sideways-communicating boxes (Figure 1-2).

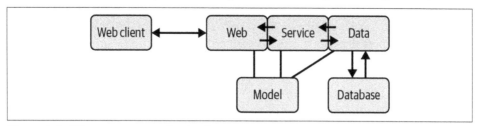

Figure 1-2. Sideways-communicating boxes

---

6 As viewers know, if your layers get sloppy, you may not return to the tent the next week.

However you visualize them, the *only* communication paths between the boxes/layers are the arrows (APIs). This is important for testing and debugging. If undocumented doors exist in a factory, the night watchman will inevitably be surprised.

The arrows between the web client and Web layer use HTTP or HTTPS to transport mostly JSON text. The arrows between the Data layer and database use a database-specific protocol and carry SQL (or other) text. The arrows between the layers themselves are function calls carrying data models.

Also, the recommended data formats flowing through the arrows are as follows:

Client ⟺ Web
    RESTful HTTP with JSON

Web ⟺ Service
    Models

Service ⟺ Data
    Models

Data ⟺ Databases and services
    Specific APIs

Based on my own experience, this is how I've chosen to structure the topics in this book. It's workable and has scaled to fairly complex sites, but isn't sacred. You may have a better design! However you do it, these are the important points:

- Separate domain-specific details.
- Define standard APIs between the layers.
- Don't cheat; don't leak.

Sometimes deciding which layer is the best home for code is a challenge. For example, Chapter 11 looks at authentication and authorization requirements and how to implement them—as an extra layer between Web and Service, or within one of them. Software development is sometimes as much art as science.

Data

The web has often been used as a frontend to relational databases, although many other ways of storing and accessing data have evolved, such as NoSQL or NewSQL databases.

But beyond databases, *machine learning (ML)*—or *deep learning* or just *AI*—is fundamentally remaking the technology landscape. The development of large models requires *lots* of messing with data, which has traditionally been called extract, transform, load (ETL).

As a general-purpose service architecture, the web can help with many of the fiddly bits of ML systems.

Review

The web uses many APIs, but especially RESTful ones. Asynchronous calls allow better concurrency, which speeds up the overall process. Web service applications are often large enough to divide into layers. Data has become a major area in its own right. All these concepts are addressed in the Python programming language, coming in the next chapter.

## CHAPTER 2

Modern Python

It's all in a day's work for Confuse-a-Cat.

—Monty Python

Preview

Python evolves to keep up with our changing technical world. This chapter discusses specific Python features that apply to issues in the previous chapter, and a few extras:

- Tools
- APIs and services
- Variables and type hinting
- Data structures
- Web frameworks

Tools

Every computing language has the following:

- The core language and built-in standard packages
- Ways to add external packages
- Recommended external packages
- An environment of development tools

The following sections list the Python tools required or recommended for this book.

These may change over time! Python packaging and development tools are moving targets, and better solutions come along now and then.

Getting Started

You should be able to write and run a Python program like Example 2-1.

Example 2-1. The Python program that goes like this: this.py

```
def paid_promotion():
    print("(that calls this function!)")

print("This is the program")
paid_promotion()
print("that goes like this.")
```

To execute this program from the command line in a text window or terminal, I'll use the convention of a $ *prompt* (your system begging you to type something, already). What you type after the prompt is shown in **bold print**. If you saved Example 2-1 to a file named *this.py*, you can run it as shown in Example 2-2.

Example 2-2. Test this.py

```
$ python this.py
This is the program
(that calls this function!)
that goes like this.
```

Some code examples use the interactive Python interpreter, which is what you get if you just type **python**:

```
$ python
Python 3.9.1 (v3.9.1:1e5d33e9b9, Dec  7 2020, 12:10:52)
[Clang 6.0 (clang-600.0.57)] on darwin
Type "help", "copyright", "credits" or "license" for more information.
>>>
```

The first few lines are specific to your operating system and Python version. The >>> is your prompt here. A handy extra feature of the interactive interpreter is that it will print the value of a variable for you if you type its name:

```
>>> wrong_answer = 43
>>> wrong_answer
43
```

This also works for expressions:

```
>>> wrong_answer = 43
>>> wrong_answer - 3
40
```

If you're fairly new to Python or would like a quick review, read the next few sections.

Python Itself

You will need, as a bare minimum, Python 3.7. This includes features like type hints and asyncio, which are core requirements for FastAPI. I recommend using at least Python 3.9, which will have a longer support lifetime. The standard source for Python is the Python Software Foundation (*https://www.python.org*).

Package Management

You will want to download external Python packages and install them safely on your computer. The classic tool for this is pip (*https://pip.pypa.io*).

But how do you download this downloader? If you installed Python from the Python Software Foundation, you should already have pip. If not, follow the instructions at the pip site to get it. Throughout this book, as I introduce a new Python package, I'll include the pip command to download it.

Although you can do a lot with plain old pip, you'll likely also want to use virtual environments and consider an alternative tool like Poetry.

Virtual Environments

Pip will download and install packages, but where should it put them? Although standard Python and its included libraries are usually installed in a standard place on your operating system, you may not (and probably should not) be able to change anything there. Pip uses a default directory other than the system one, so you won't step on your system's standard Python files. You can change this; see the pip site for details for your operating system.

But it's common to work with multiple versions of Python, or make installations specific to a project, so you know exactly which packages are in there. To do this, Python supports *virtual environments*. These are just directories (*folders* in the non-Unix world) into which pip writes downloaded packages. When you *activate* a virtual environment, your shell (main system command interpreter) looks there first when loading Python modules.

The program for this is venv (*https://oreil.ly/9kv5T*), and it's been included with standard Python since version 3.4.

Let's make a virtual environment called `venv1`. You can run the venv module as a standalone program:

```
$ venv venv1
```

Or as a Python module:

```
$ python -m venv venv1
```

To make this your current Python environment, run this shell command (on Linux or Mac; see the venv docs for Windows and others):

```
$ source venv1/bin/activate
```

Now, anytime you run `pip install`, it will install packages under `venv1`. And when you run Python programs, that's where your Python interpreter and modules will be found.

To *de*activate your virtual environment, press Control-D (Linux or Mac), or type **deactivate** (Windows).

You can create alternative environments like `venv2`, and deactivate/activate to step between them (although I hope you have more naming imagination than me).

Poetry

This combination of pip and venv is so common that people started combining them to save steps and avoid that `source` shell wizardry. One such package is Pipenv (*https://pipenv.pypa.io*), but a newer rival called Poetry (*https://python-poetry.org*) is becoming more popular.

Having used pip, Pipenv, and Poetry, I now prefer Poetry. Get it with `pip install poetry`. Poetry has many subcommands, such as `poetry add` to add a package to your virtual environment, `poetry install` to actually download and install it, and so on. Check the Poetry site or run the `poetry` command for help.

Besides downloading single packages, pip and Poetry manage multiple packages in configuration files: *requirements.txt* for pip, and *pyproject.toml* for Poetry. Poetry and pip don't just download packages, but also manage the tricky dependencies that packages may have on other packages. You can specify desired package versions as minima, maxima, ranges, or exact values (also known as *pinning*). This can be important as your project grows and the packages that it depends on change. You may need a minimum version of a package if a feature that you use first appeared there, or a maximum if a feature was dropped.

Source Formatting

Source formatting is less important than the topics of the previous sections but still helpful. Avoid code formatting (*bikeshedding*) arguments with a tool that massages source into a standard, nonweird format. One good choice is Black (*https://black.read thedocs.io*). Install it with `pip install black`.

Testing

Testing is covered in detail in Chapter 12. Although the standard Python test package is unittest, the industrial-strength Python test package used by most Python developers is pytest (*https://docs.pytest.org*). Install it with `pip install pytest`.

Source Control and Continuous Integration

The almost-universal solution for source control now is *Git*, with storage repositories (*repos*) at sites like GitHub and GitLab. Using Git isn't specific to Python or FastAPI, but you'll likely spend a lot of your development time with Git. The pre-commit (*https://pre-commit.com*) tool runs various tests on your local machine (such as `black` and `pytest`) before committing to Git. After pushing to a remote Git repo, more continuous integration (CI) tests may be run there.

Chapter 12 and "Troubleshooting" on page 190 have more details.

Web Tools

Chapter 3 shows how to install and use the main Python web tools used in this book:

FastAPI
    The web framework itself

Uvicorn
    An asynchronous web server

HTTPie
    A text web client, similar to curl

Requests
    A synchronous web client package

HTTPX
    A synchronous/asynchronous web client package

APIs and Services

Python's modules and packages are essential for creating large applications that don't become "big balls of mud" (*https://oreil.ly/zzX5T*). Even in a single-process web service, you can maintain the separation discussed in Chapter 1 by the careful design of modules and imports.

Python's built-in data structures are extremely flexible, and very tempting to use everywhere. But in the coming chapters, you'll see that we can define higher-level *models* to make our interlayer communication cleaner. These models rely on a fairly recent Python addition called *type hinting*. Let's get into that, but first with a brief aside on how Python handles *variables*. This won't hurt.

Variables Are Names

The term *object* has many definitions in the software world—maybe too many. In Python, an object is a data structure that wraps every distinct piece of data in the program, from an integer like 5, to a function, to anything that you might define. It specifies, among other bookkeeping info, the following:

- A unique *identity* value
- The low-level *type* that matches the hardware
- The specific *value* (physical bits)
- A *reference count* of the number of variables that refer to it

Python is *strongly typed* at the object level (its *type* doesn't change, although its *value* might). An object is termed *mutable* if its value may be changed, *immutable* if not.

But at the *variable* level, Python differs from many other computing languages, and this can be confusing. In many other languages, a *variable* is essentially a direct pointer to an area of memory that contains a raw *value*, stored in bits that follow the computer's hardware design. If you assign a new value to that variable, the language overwrites the previous value in memory with the new one.

That's direct and fast. The compiler keeps track of what goes where. It's one reason languages like C are faster than Python. As a developer, you need to ensure that you assign only values of the correct type to each variable.

Now, here's the big difference with Python: a Python variable is just a *name* that is temporarily associated with a higher-level *object* in memory. If you assign a new value to a variable that refers to an immutable object, you're actually creating a new object that contains that value, and then getting the name to refer to that new object. The old object (that the name used to refer to) is then free, and its memory can be reclaimed if no other names are still referring to it (i.e., its reference count is 0).

In *Introducing Python* (O'Reilly), I compare objects to plastic boxes sitting on memory shelves, and names/variables to sticky notes on these boxes. Or you can picture names as tags attached by strings to those boxes.

Usually, when you use a name, you assign it to one object, and it stays attached. Such simple consistency helps you understand your code. A variable's *scope* is the area of code in which a name refers to the same object—such as within a function. You can use the same name in different scopes, but each one refers to a different object.

Although you can make a variable refer to different objects throughout a Python program, that isn't necessarily a good practice. Without looking, you don't know if name x on line 100 is in the same scope as name x on line 20. (By the way, x is a terrible name. We should pick names that actually confer some meaning.)

Type Hints

All of this background has a point.

Python 3.6 added *type hints* to declare the type of object to which a variable refers. These are *not* enforced by the Python interpreter as it's running! Instead, they can be used by various tools to ensure that your use of a variable is consistent. The standard type checker is called *mypy*, and I'll show you how it's used later.

A type hint may seem like just a nice thing, like many lint tools used by programmers to avoid mistakes. For instance, it may remind you that your variable count refers to a Python object of type int. But hints, although they're optional and unenforced notes (literally, hints), turn out to have unexpected uses. Later in this book, you'll see how FastAPI adapted the Pydantic package to make clever use of type hinting.

The addition of type declarations may be a trend in other, formerly typeless, languages. For example, many JavaScript developers have moved to TypeScript (*https://www.typescriptlang.org*).

Data Structures

You'll get details on Python and data structures in Chapter 5.

Web Frameworks

Among other things, a web framework translates between HTTP bytes and Python data structures. It can save you a lot of effort. On the other hand, if part of it doesn't work as you need it to, you may need to hack a solution. As the saying goes, don't reinvent the wheel—unless you can't get a round one.

The Web Server Gateway Interface (WSGI) (*https://wsgi.readthedocs.io*) is a synchronous Python standard specification (*https://peps.python.org/pep-3333*) to connect application code to web servers. Traditional Python web frameworks are all built on WSGI. But synchronous communication may mean busy waiting for something that's *much* slower than the CPU, like a disk or network. Then you'll look for better *concurrency*. Concurrency has become more important in recent years. As a result, the Python Asynchronous Server Gateway Interface (ASGI) specification (*https://asgi.readthedocs.io*) was developed. Chapter 4 talks about this.

Django

Django (*https://www.djangoproject.com*) is a full-featured web framework that tags itself as "the web framework for perfectionists with deadlines." It was announced by Adrian Holovaty and Simon Willison in 2003, and named after Django Reinhardt, a 20th-century Belgian jazz guitarist. Django is often used for database-backed corporate sites. I include more details on Django in Chapter 7.

Flask

In contrast, Flask (*https://flask.palletsprojects.com*), introduced by Armin Ronacher in 2010, is a *microframework*. Chapter 7 has more information on Flask and how it compares with Django and FastAPI.

FastAPI

After meeting other suitors at the ball, we finally encounter the intriguing FastAPI, the subject of this book. Although FastAPI was published by Sebastián Ramírez in 2018, it has already climbed to the third place of Python web frameworks, behind Flask and Django, and is growing faster. A 2022 comparison (*https://oreil.ly/36WTQ*) shows that it may pass them at some point.

As of the end of October 2023, here are the GitHub star counts:

- Django: 73.8 thousand
- Flask: 64.8 thousand
- FastAPI: 64 thousand

After careful investigation into alternatives (*https://oreil.ly/JDDOm*), Ramírez came up with a design (*https://oreil.ly/zJFTX*) that was heavily based on two third-party Python packages:

- *Starlette* for web details
- *Pydantic* for data details

And he added his own ingredients and special sauces to the final product. You'll see what I mean in the next chapter.

Review

This chapter covered a lot of ground related to today's Python:

- Useful tools for a Python web developer
- The prominence of APIs and services
- Python's type hinting, objects, and variables
- Data structures for web services
- Web frameworks

## PART II

A FastAPI Tour

The chapters in this part provide a thousand-foot view of FastAPI—more like a drone than a spy satellite. They cover the basics quickly but stay above the water line to avoid drowning you in details. The chapters are relatively short and are meant to provide context for the depths of Part III.

After you get used to the ideas in this part, Part III zooms into those details. That's where you can do some serious good, or damage. No judgment; it's up to you.

## CHAPTER 3

FastAPI Tour

FastAPI is a modern, fast (high-performance) web framework for building APIs with Python 3.6+ based on standard Python type hints.

—Sebastián Ramírez, creator of FastAPI

Preview

FastAPI (*https://fastapi.tiangolo.com*) was announced in 2018 by Sebastián Ramírez (*https://tiangolo.com*). It's more modern in many senses than most Python web frameworks—taking advantage of features that have been added to Python 3 in the last few years. This chapter is a quick overview of FastAPI's main features, with emphasis on the first things that you'll want to know: how to handle web requests and responses.

What Is FastAPI?

Like any web framework, FastAPI helps you build web applications. Every framework is designed to make some operations easier—by features, omissions, and defaults. As the name implies, FastAPI targets development of web APIs, although you can use it for traditional web content applications as well.

The FastAPI website claims these advantages:

Performance
   As fast as Node.js and Go in some cases, unusual for Python frameworks.

Faster development
   No sharp edges or oddities.

Better code quality
   Type hinting and models help reduce bugs.

Autogenerated documentation and test pages
Much easier than hand-editing OpenAPI descriptions.

FastAPI uses the following:

- Python type hints
- Starlette for the web machinery, including async support
- Pydantic for data definitions and validation
- Special integration to leverage and extend the others

This combination makes a pleasing development environment for web applications, especially RESTful web services.

A FastAPI Application

Let's write a teeny FastAPI application—a web service with a single endpoint. For now, we're in what I've called the Web layer, handling only web requests and responses. First, install the basic Python packages that we'll be using:

- The FastAPI (*https://fastapi.tiangolo.com*) framework: `pip install fastapi`
- The Uvicorn (*https://www.uvicorn.org*) web server: `pip install uvicorn`
- The HTTPie (*https://httpie.io*) text web client: `pip install httpie`
- The Requests (*https://requests.readthedocs.io*) synchronous web client package: `pip install requests`
- The HTTPX (*https://www.python-httpx.org*) synchronous/asynchronous web client package: `pip install httpx`

Although curl (*https://curl.se*) is the best known text web client, I think HTTPie is easier to use. Also, it defaults to JSON encoding and decoding, which is a better match for FastAPI. Later in this chapter, you'll see a screenshot that includes the syntax of the curl command line needed to access a particular endpoint.

Let's shadow an introverted web developer in Example 3-1 and save this code as the file *hello.py*.

Example 3-1. A shy endpoint (hello.py)

```
from fastapi import FastAPI

app = FastAPI()

@app.get("/hi")
```

```
def greet():
    return "Hello? World?"
```

Here are some points to notice:

- app is the top-level FastAPI object that represents the whole web application.
- @app.get("/hi") is a *path decorator*. It tells FastAPI the following:
  — A request for the URL "/hi" on this server should be directed to the following function.
  — This decorator applies only to the HTTP GET verb. You can also respond to a "/hi" URL sent with the other HTTP verbs (PUT, POST, etc.), each with a separate function.
- def greet() is a *path function*—the main point of contact with HTTP requests and responses. In this example, it has no arguments, but the following sections show that there's much more under the FastAPI hood.

The next step is to run this web application in a web server. FastAPI itself does not include a web server but recommends Uvicorn. You can start Uvicorn and the FastAPI web application in two ways: externally or internally.

To start Uvicorn externally, via the command line, see Example 3-2.

Example 3-2. Start Uvicorn with the command line

```
$ uvicorn hello:app --reload
```

The hello refers to the *hello.py* file, and app is the FastAPI variable name within it.

Alternatively, you can start Uvicorn internally in the application itself, as in Example 3-3.

Example 3-3. Start Uvicorn internally

```
from fastapi import FastAPI

app = FastAPI()

@app.get("/hi")
def greet():
    return "Hello? World?"

if __name__ == "__main__":
    import uvicorn
    uvicorn.run("hello:app", reload=True)
```

In either case, that `reload` tells Uvicorn to restart the web server if *hello.py* changes. In this chapter, we're going to use this automatic reloading a lot.

Either case will use port 8000 on your machine (named `localhost`) by default. Both the external and internal methods have `host` and `port` arguments if you'd prefer something else.

Now the server has a single endpoint (*/hi*) and is ready for requests.

Let's test with multiple web clients:

- For the browser, type the URL in the top location bar.
- For HTTPie, type the command shown (the `$` stands for whatever command prompt you have for your system shell).
- For Requests or HTTPX, use Python in interactive mode, and type after the `>>>` prompt.

As mentioned in the Preface, what you type is in a

    bold monospaced font

and the output is in a

    `normal monospaced font`

Examples 3-4 through 3-7 show different ways to test the web server's brand-new */hi* endpoint.

Example 3-4. Test /hi in the browser

```
http://localhost:8000/hi
```

Example 3-5. Test /hi with Requests

```
>>> import requests
>>> r = requests.get("http://localhost:8000/hi")
>>> r.json()
'Hello? World?'
```

Example 3-6. Test /hi with HTTPX, which is almost identical to Requests

```
>>> import httpx
>>> r = httpx.get("http://localhost:8000/hi")
>>> r.json()
'Hello? World?'
```

It doesn't matter if you use Requests or HTTPX to test FastAPI routes. But Chapter 13 shows cases where HTTPX is useful when making other asynchronous calls. So the rest of the examples in this chapter use Requests.

Example 3-7. Test /hi with HTTPie

```
$ http localhost:8000/hi
HTTP/1.1 200 OK
content-length: 15
content-type: application/json
date: Thu, 30 Jun 2022 07:38:27 GMT
server: uvicorn

"Hello? World?"
```

Use the -b argument in Example 3-8 to skip the response headers and print only the body.

Example 3-8. Test /hi with HTTPie, printing only the response body

```
$ http -b localhost:8000/hi
"Hello? World?"
```

Example 3-9 gets the full request headers as well as the response with -v.

Example 3-9. Test /hi with HTTPie and get everything

```
$ http -v localhost:8000/hi
GET /hi HTTP/1.1
Accept: /
Accept-Encoding: gzip, deflate
Connection: keep-alive
Host: localhost:8000
User-Agent: HTTPie/3.2.1


HTTP/1.1 200 OK
content-length: 15
content-type: application/json
date: Thu, 30 Jun 2022 08:05:06 GMT
server: uvicorn

"Hello? World?"
```

Some examples in this book show the default HTTPie output (response headers and body), and others show just the body.

HTTP Requests

Example 3-9 included only one specific request: a GET request for the */hi* URL on the server localhost, port 8000.

Web requests squirrel data in different parts of an HTTP request, and FastAPI lets you access them smoothly. From the sample request in Example 3-9, Example 3-10 shows the HTTP request that the http command sent to the web server.

Example 3-10. An HTTP request

```
GET /hi HTTP/1.1
Accept: /
Accept-Encoding: gzip, deflate
Connection: keep-alive
Host: localhost:8000
User-Agent: HTTPie/3.2.1
```

This request contains the following:

- The verb (GET) and path (/hi)
- Any *query parameters* (text after any ? in this case, none)
- Other HTTP headers
- No request body content

FastAPI unsquirrels these into handy definitions:

Header
  The HTTP headers

Path
  The URL

Query
  The query parameters (after the ? at the end of the URL)

Body
  The HTTP body

The way that FastAPI provides data from various parts of the HTTP requests is one of its best features and an improvement on how most Python web frameworks do it. All the arguments that you need can be declared and provided directly inside the path function, using the definitions in the preceding list (Path, Query, etc.), and by functions that you write. This uses a technique called *dependency injection*, which will be discussed as we go along and expanded on in Chapter 6.

Let's make our earlier application a little more personal by adding a parameter called who that addresses that plaintive Hello? to someone. We'll try different ways to pass this new parameter:

- In the URL *path*
- As a *query* parameter, after the ? in the URL
- In the HTTP *body*
- As an HTTP *header*

URL Path

Edit *hello.py* in Example 3-11.

Example 3-11. Return the greeting path

```
from fastapi import FastAPI

app = FastAPI()

@app.get("/hi/{who}")
def greet(who):
    return f"Hello? {who}?"
```

Once you save this change from your editor, Uvicorn should restart. (Otherwise, we'd create *hello2.py*, etc. and rerun Uvicorn each time.) If you have a typo, keep trying until you fix it, and Uvicorn won't give you a hard time.

Adding that {who} in the URL (after @app.get) tells FastAPI to expect a variable named who at that position in the URL. FastAPI then assigns it to the who argument in the following greet() function. This shows coordination between the path decorator and the path function.

Do not use a Python f-string for the amended URL string (`"/hi/{who}"`) here. The curly brackets are used by FastAPI itself to match URL pieces as path parameters.

In Examples 3-12 through 3-14, test this modified endpoint with the various methods discussed earlier.

Example 3-12. Test /hi/Mom in the browser

```
localhost:8000/hi/Mom
```

Example 3-13. Test /hi/Mom with HTTPie

```
$ http localhost:8000/hi/Mom
HTTP/1.1 200 OK
content-length: 13
content-type: application/json
date: Thu, 30 Jun 2022 08:09:02 GMT
server: uvicorn

"Hello? Mom?"
```

Example 3-14. Test /hi/Mom with Requests

```
>>> import requests
>>> r = requests.get("http://localhost:8000/hi/Mom")
>>> r.json()
'Hello? Mom?'
```

In each case, the string `"Mom"` is passed as part of the URL, passed to the `greet()` path function as the `who` variable, and returned as part of the response.

The response in each case is the JSON string (with single or double quotes, depending on which test client you used) `"Hello? Mom?"`.

Query Parameters

Query parameters are the *name=value* strings after the ? in a URL, separated by & characters. Edit *hello.py* again in Example 3-15.

Example 3-15. Return the greeting query parameter

```
from fastapi import FastAPI

app = FastAPI()
```

```
@app.get("/hi")
def greet(who):
    return f"Hello? {who}?"
```

The endpoint function is defined as greet(who) again, but {who} isn't in the URL on the previous decorator line this time, so FastAPI now assumes that who is a query parameter. Test with Examples 3-16 and 3-17.

Example 3-16. Test Example 3-15 with your browser

```
localhost:8000/hi?who=Mom
```

Example 3-17. Test Example 3-15 with HTTPie

```
$ http -b localhost:8000/hi?who=Mom
"Hello? Mom?"
```

In Example 3-18, you can call HTTPie with a query parameter argument (note the ==).

Example 3-18. Test Example 3-15 with HTTPie and params

```
$ http -b localhost:8000/hi who==Mom
"Hello? Mom?"
```

You can have more than one of these arguments for HTTPie, and it's easier to type these as space-separated arguments.

Examples 3-19 and 3-20 show the same alternatives for Requests.

Example 3-19. Test Example 3-15 with Requests

```
>>> import requests
>>> r = requests.get("http://localhost:8000/hi?who=Mom")
>>> r.json()
'Hello? Mom?'
```

Example 3-20. Test Example 3-15 with Requests and params

```
>>> import requests
>>> params = {"who": "Mom"}
>>> r = requests.get("http://localhost:8000/hi", params=params)
>>> r.json()
'Hello? Mom?'
```

In each case, you provide the "Mom" string in a new way, and get it to the path function and through to the eventual response.

Body

We can provide path or query parameters to a GET endpoint, but not values from the request body. In HTTP, GET is supposed to be *idempotent*—a computery term for *ask the same question, get the same answer*. HTTP GET is supposed to only return stuff. The request body is used to send stuff to the server when creating (POST) or updating (PUT or PATCH). Chapter 9 shows a way around this.

So, in Example 3-21, let's change the endpoint from a GET to a POST. (Technically, we're not creating anything, so a POST isn't kosher, but if the RESTful Overlords sue us, then hey, check out the cool courthouse.)

Example 3-21. Return the greeting body

```
from fastapi import FastAPI, Body

app = FastAPI()

@app.post("/hi")
def greet(who:str = Body(embed=True)):
    return f"Hello? {who}?"
```

 That Body(embed=True) is needed to tell FastAPI that, this time, we get the value of who from the JSON-formatted request body. The embed part means that it should look like {"who": "Mom"} rather than just "Mom".

Try testing with HTTPie in Example 3-22, using -v to show the generated request body (and note the single = parameter to indicate JSON body data).

Example 3-22. Test Example 3-21 with HTTPie

```
$ http -v localhost:8000/hi who=Mom
POST /hi HTTP/1.1
Accept: application/json, /;q=0.5
Accept-Encoding: gzip, deflate
Connection: keep-alive
Content-Length: 14
Content-Type: application/json
Host: localhost:8000
User-Agent: HTTPie/3.2.1
```

```
{
    "who": "Mom"
}
```

```
HTTP/1.1 200 OK
content-length: 13
content-type: application/json
date: Thu, 30 Jun 2022 08:37:00 GMT
server: uvicorn

"Hello? Mom?"
```

And finally, test with Requests in Example 3-23, which uses its `json` argument to pass JSON-encoded data in the request body.

Example 3-23. Test Example 3-21 with Requests

```
>>> import requests
>>> r = requests.post("http://localhost:8000/hi", json={"who": "Mom"})
>>> r.json()
'Hello? Mom?'
```

HTTP Header

Finally, let's try passing the greeting argument as an HTTP header in Example 3-24.

Example 3-24. Return the greeting header

```
from fastapi import FastAPI, Header

app = FastAPI()

@app.post("/hi")
def greet(who:str = Header()):
    return f"Hello? {who}?"
```

Let's test this one just with HTTPie in Example 3-25. It uses *name:value* to specify an HTTP header.

Example 3-25. Test Example 3-24 with HTTPie

```
$ http -v localhost:8000/hi who:Mom
GET /hi HTTP/1.1
Accept: */\*
Accept-Encoding: gzip, deflate
Connection: keep-alive
Host: localhost:8000
User-Agent: HTTPie/3.2.1
```

```
who: Mom

HTTP/1.1 200 OK
content-length: 13
content-type: application/json
date: Mon, 16 Jan 2023 05:14:46 GMT
server: uvicorn

"Hello? Mom?"
```

FastAPI converts HTTP header keys to lowercase, and converts a hyphen (-) to an underscore (_). So you could print the value of the HTTP User-Agent header like this in Examples 3-26 and 3-27.

Example 3-26. Return the User-Agent header (hello.py)

```python
from fastapi import FastAPI, Header

app = FastAPI()

@app.post("/agent")
def get_agent(user_agent:str = Header()):
    return user_agent
```

Example 3-27. Test the User-Agent header with HTTPie

```
$ http -v localhost:8000/agent
GET /agent HTTP/1.1
Accept: */\*
Accept-Encoding: gzip, deflate
Connection: keep-alive
Host: localhost:8000
User-Agent: HTTPie/3.2.1


HTTP/1.1 200 OK
content-length: 14
content-type: application/json
date: Mon, 16 Jan 2023 05:21:35 GMT
server: uvicorn

"HTTPie/3.2.1"
```

Multiple Request Data

You can use more than one of these methods in the same path function. That is, you can get data from the URL, query parameters, the HTTP body, HTTP headers, cookies, and so on. And you can write your own dependency functions that process and combine them in special ways, such as for pagination or authentication. You'll see some of these in Chapter 6 and in various chapters in Part III.

Which Method Is Best?

Here are a few recommendations:

- When passing arguments in the URL, following RESTful guidelines is standard practice.
- Query strings are usually used to provide optional arguments, like pagination.
- The body is usually used for larger inputs, like whole or partial models.

In each case, if you provide type hints in your data definitions, your arguments will be automatically type-checked by Pydantic. This ensures that they're both present and correct.

HTTP Responses

By default, FastAPI converts whatever you return from your endpoint function to JSON; the HTTP response has a header line `Content-type: application/json`. So, although the `greet()` function initially returns the string `"Hello? World?"`, FastAPI converts it to JSON. This is one of the defaults chosen by FastAPI to streamline API development.

In this case, the Python string `"Hello? World?"` is converted to its equivalent JSON string `"Hello? World?"`, which is the same darn string. But anything that you return is converted to JSON, whether built-in Python types or Pydantic models.

Status Code

By default, FastAPI returns a 200 status code; exceptions raise 4xx codes.

In the path decorator, specify the HTTP status code that should be returned if all goes well (exceptions will generate their own codes and override it). Add the code from Example 3-28 somewhere in your *hello.py* (just to avoid showing the whole file again and again), and test it with Example 3-29.

Example 3-28. Specify the HTTP status code (add to hello.py*)*

```
@app.get("/happy")
def happy(status_code=200):
    return ":)"
```

Example 3-29. Test the HTTP status code

```
$ http localhost:8000/happy
HTTP/1.1 200 OK
content-length: 4
content-type: application/json
date: Sun, 05 Feb 2023 04:37:32 GMT
server: uvicorn

":)"
```

Headers

You can inject HTTP response headers, as in Example 3-30 (you don't need to return response).

Example 3-30. Set the HTTP headers (add to hello.py)

```
from fastapi import Response

@app.get("/header/{name}/{value}")
def header(name: str, value: str, response:Response):
    response.headers[name] = value
    return "normal body"
```

Let's see if it worked (Example 3-31).

Example 3-31. Test the response HTTP headers

```
$ http localhost:8000/header/marco/polo
HTTP/1.1 200 OK
content-length: 13
content-type: application/json
date: Wed, 31 May 2023 17:47:38 GMT
marco: polo
server: uvicorn

"normal body"
```

Response Types

Response types (import these classes from `fastapi.responses`) include the following:

- `JSONResponse` (the default)
- `HTMLResponse`
- `PlainTextResponse`

- `RedirectResponse`
- `FileResponse`
- `StreamingResponse`

I'll say more about the last two in Chapter 15.

For other output formats (also known as *MIME types*), you can use a generic `Response` class, which needs the following:

`content`
String or bytes

`media_type`
The string MIME type

`status_code`
HTTP integer status code

`headers`
A `dict` of strings

Type Conversion

The path function can return anything, and by default (using `JSONResponse`), FastAPI will convert it to a JSON string and return it, with the matching HTTP response headers `Content-Length` and `Content-Type`. This includes any Pydantic model class.

But how does it do this? If you've used the Python json library, you've probably seen that it raises an exception when given some data types, such as `datetime`. FastAPI uses an internal function called `jsonable_encoder()` to convert any data structure to a "JSONable" Python data structure, then calls the usual `json.dumps()` to turn that into a JSON string. Example 3-32 shows a test that you can run with pytest.

Example 3-32. Use `jsonable_encoder()` to avoid JSON kabooms

```
import datetime
import pytest
from fastapi.encoders import jsonable_encoder
import json

@pytest.fixture
def data():
    return datetime.datetime.now()

def test_json_dump(data):
    with pytest.raises(Exception):
        _ = json.dumps(data)
```

```
def test_encoder(data):
    out = jsonable_encoder(data)
    assert out
    json_out = json.dumps(out)
    assert json_out
```

Model Types and response_model

It's possible to have different classes with many of the same fields, except one is specialized for user input, one for output, and one for internal use. Some reasons for these variants could include the following:

- Remove some sensitive information from the output—like *deidentifying* personal medical data, if you've encountered Health Insurance Portability and Accountability Act (HIPAA) requirements.
- Add fields to the user input (like a creation date and time).

Example 3-33 shows three related classes for a contrived case:

- TagIn is the class that defines what the user needs to provide (in this case, just a string called tag).
- Tag is made from a TagIn and adds two fields: created (when this Tag was created) and secret (an internal string, maybe stored in a database, but never supposed to be exposed to the world).
- TagOut is the class that defines what can be returned to a user (by a lookup or search endpoint). It contains the tag field from the original TagIn object and its derived Tag object, plus the created field generated for Tag, but not secret.

Example 3-33. Model variations (model/tag.py)

```
from datetime import datetime
from pydantic import BaseClass

class TagIn(BaseClass):
    tag: str

class Tag(BaseClass):
    tag: str
    created: datetime
    secret: str

class TagOut(BaseClass):
    tag: str
    created: datetime
```

You can return data types other than the default JSON from a FastAPI path function in different ways. One method is to use the `response_model` argument in the path decorator to goose FastAPI to return something else. FastAPI will drop any fields that were in the object that you returned but are not in the object specified by `response_model`.

In Example 3-34, pretend that you wrote a new service module called *service/tag.py* with the `create()` and `get()` functions that give this web module something to call. Those lower-stack details don't matter here. The important point is the `get_one()` path function at the bottom, and the `response_model=TagOut` in its path decorator. That automatically changes an internal `Tag` object to a sanitized `TagOut` object.

Example 3-34. Return a different response type with `response_model` (web/tag.py)

```
import datetime
from model.tag import TagIn, Tag, TagOut
import service.tag as service

@app.post('/')
def create(tag_in: TagIn) -> TagIn:
    tag: Tag = Tag(tag=tag_in.tag, created=datetime.utcnow(),
        secret="shhhh")
    service.create(tag)
    return tag_in

@app.get('/{tag_str}', response_model=TagOut)
def get_one(tag_str: str) -> TagOut:
    tag: Tag = service.get(tag_str)
    return tag
```

Even though we returned a `Tag`, `response_model` will convert it to a `TagOut`.

Automated Documentation

This section assumes that you're running the web application from Example 3-21, the version that sends the who parameter in the HTTP body via a POST request to *http://localhost:8000/hi*.

Convince your browser to visit the URL **http://localhost:8000/docs**.

You'll see something that starts like Figure 3-1 (I've cropped the following screenshots to emphasize particular areas).

Figure 3-1. Generated documentation page

Where did that come from?

FastAPI generates an OpenAPI specification from your code, and includes this page to display *and test* all your endpoints. This is just one ingredient of its secret sauce.

Click the down arrow on the right side of the green box to open it for testing (Figure 3-2).

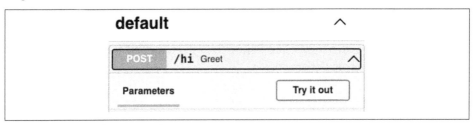

Figure 3-2. Open documentation page

Click that "Try it out" button on the right. Now you'll see an area that will let you enter a value in the body section (Figure 3-3).

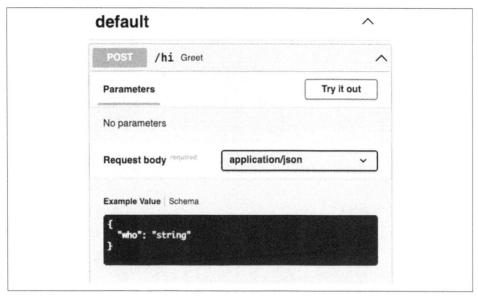

Figure 3-3. Data entry page

Click that "string". Change it to **"Cousin Eddie"** (keep the double quotes around it). Then click the bottom blue Execute button.

Now look at the Responses section below the Execute button (Figure 3-4).

The "Response body" box shows that Cousin Eddie turned up.

So, this is yet another way to test the site (besides the earlier examples using the browser, HTTPie, and Requests).

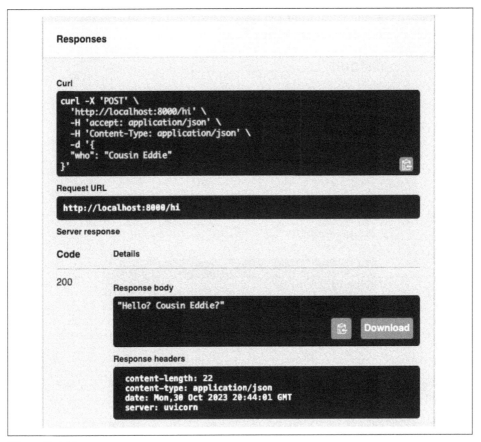

Figure 3-4. Response page

By the way, as you can see in the Curl box of the Responses display, using curl for command-line testing instead of HTTPie would have required more typing. HTTPie's automatic JSON encoding helps here.

This automated documentation is actually a big, furry deal. As your web service grows to hundreds of endpoints, a documentation and testing page that's always up-to-date is helpful.

Complex Data

These examples showed only how to pass a single string to an endpoint. Many endpoints, especially GET or DELETE ones, may need no arguments at all, or only a few simple ones, like strings and numbers. But when creating (POST) or modifying (PUT or PATCH) a resource, we usually need more complex data structures. Chapter 5 shows how FastAPI uses Pydantic and data models to implement these cleanly.

Review

In this chapter, we used FastAPI to create a website with a single endpoint. Multiple web clients tested it: a web browser, the HTTPie text program, the Requests Python package, and the HTTPX Python package. Starting with a simple GET call, request arguments went to the server via the URL path, a query parameter, and an HTTP header. Then, the HTTP body was used to send data to a POST endpoint. Later, the chapter showed how to return various HTTP response types. Finally, an automatically generated form page provided both documentation and live forms for a fourth test client.

This FastAPI overview will be expanded in Chapter 8.

## CHAPTER 4

Async, Concurrency, and Starlette Tour

> Starlette is a lightweight ASGI framework/toolkit, which is ideal for building async web services in Python.
>
> —Tom Christie, creator of Starlette

Preview

The previous chapter briefly introduced the first things a developer would encounter on writing a new FastAPI application. This chapter emphasizes FastAPI's underlying Starlette library, particularly its support of *async* processing. After an overview of multiple ways of "doing more things at once" in Python, you'll see how its newer `async` and `await` keywords have been incorporated into Starlette and FastAPI.

Starlette

Much of FastAPI's web code is based on the Starlette package (*https://www.star lette.io*), which was created by Tom Christie. It can be used as a web framework in its own right or as a library for other frameworks, such as FastAPI. Like any other web framework, Starlette handles all the usual HTTP request parsing and response generation. It's similar to Werkzeug (*https://werkzeug.palletsprojects.com*), the package that underlies Flask.

But its most important feature is its support of the modern Python asynchronous web standard: ASGI (*https://asgi.readthedocs.io*). Until now, most Python web frameworks (like Flask and Django) have been based on the traditional synchronous WSGI standard (*https://wsgi.readthedocs.io*). Because web applications so frequently connect to much slower code (e.g., database, file, and network access), ASGI avoids the blocking and busy waiting of WSGI-based applications.

As a result, Starlette and frameworks that use it are the fastest Python web packages, rivaling even Go and Node.js applications.

Types of Concurrency

Before getting into the details of the *async* support provided by Starlette and FastAPI, it's useful to know the multiple ways we can implement *concurrency*.

In *parallel* computing, a task is spread across multiple dedicated CPUs at the same time. This is common in "number-crunching" applications like graphics and machine learning.

In *concurrent* computing, each CPU switches among multiple tasks. Some tasks take longer than others, and we want to reduce the total time needed. Reading a file or accessing a remote network service is literally thousands to millions of times slower than running calculations in the CPU.

Web applications do a lot of this slow work. How can we make web servers, or any servers, run faster? This section discusses some possibilities, from system-wide down to the focus of this chapter: FastAPI's implementation of Python's `async` and `await`.

Distributed and Parallel Computing

If you have a really big application—one that would huff and puff on a single CPU—you can break it into pieces and make those pieces run on separate CPUs in a single machine or on multiple machines. You can do this in many, many ways, and if you have such an application, you already know a number of them. Managing all these pieces is more complex and expensive than managing a single server.

In this book, the focus is on small- to medium-sized applications that could fit on a single box. And these applications can have a mixture of synchronous and asynchronous code, nicely managed by FastAPI.

Operating System Processes

An operating system (or *OS*, because typing hurts) schedules resources: memory, CPUs, devices, networks, and so on. Every program that it runs executes its code in one or more *processes*. The OS provides each process with managed, protected access to resources, including when they can use the CPU.

Most systems use *preemptive* process scheduling, not allowing any process to hog the CPU, memory, or any other resource. An OS continually suspends and resumes processes, according to its design and settings.

For developers, the good news is: not your problem! But the bad news (which usually seems to shadow the good) is: you can't do much to change it, even if you want to.

With CPU-intensive Python applications, the usual solution is to use multiple processes and let the OS manage them. Python has a multiprocessing module (*https:// oreil.ly/YO4YE*) for this.

Operating System Threads

You can also run *threads* of control within a single process. Python's threading package (*https://oreil.ly/xwVB1*) manages these.

Threads are often recommended when your program is I/O bound, and multiple processes are recommended when you're CPU bound. But threads are tricky to program and can cause errors that are hard to find. In *Introducing Python*, I likened threads to ghosts wafting around in a haunted house: independent and invisible, detected only by their effects. Hey, who moved that candlestick?

Traditionally, Python kept the process-based and thread-based libraries separate. Developers had to learn the arcane details of either to use them. A more recent package called concurrent.futures (*https://oreil.ly/dT150*) is a higher-level interface that makes them easier to use.

As you'll see, you can get the benefits of threads more easily with the newer async functions. FastAPI also manages threads for normal synchronous functions (def, not async def) via threadpools.

Green Threads

A more mysterious mechanism is presented by *green threads* such as greenlet (*https:// greenlet.readthedocs.io*), gevent (*http://www.gevent.org*) and Eventlet (*https://event let.net*). These are *cooperative* (not preemptive). They're similar to OS threads but run in user space (i.e., your program) rather than in the OS kernel. They work by *monkey-patching* standard Python functions (modifying standard Python functions as they're running) to make concurrent code look like normal sequential code: they give up control when they would block waiting for I/O.

OS threads are "lighter" (use less memory) than OS processes, and green threads are lighter than OS threads. In some benchmarks (*https://oreil.ly/1NFYb*), all the async methods were generally faster than their sync counterparts.

 After you've read this chapter, you may wonder which is better: gevent or asyncio? I don't think there's a single preference for all uses. Green threads were implemented earlier (using ideas from the multiplayer game *Eve Online*). This book features Python's standard asyncio, which is used by FastAPI, is simpler than threads, and performs well.

Callbacks

Developers of interactive applications like games and graphic user interfaces are probably familiar with *callbacks*. You write functions and associate them with an event, like a mouse click, keypress, or time. The prominent Python package in this category is Twisted (*https://twisted.org*). Its name reflects the reality that callback-based programs are a bit "inside-out" and hard to follow.

Python Generators

Like most languages, Python usually executes code sequentially. When you call a function, Python runs it from its first line until its end or a `return`.

But in a Python *generator function*, you can stop and return from any point, *and go back to that point* later. The trick is the `yield` keyword.

In one *Simpsons* episode, Homer crashes his car into a deer statue, followed by three lines of dialogue. Example 4-1 defines a normal Python function to `return` these lines as a list and have the caller iterate over them.

Example 4-1. Use `return`

```
>>> def doh():
...     return ["Homer: D'oh!", "Marge: A deer!", "Lisa: A female deer!"]
...
>>> for line in doh():
...     print(line)
...
Homer: D'oh!
Marge: A deer!
Lisa: A female deer!
```

This works perfectly when lists are relatively small. But what if we're grabbing all the dialogue from all the *Simpsons* episodes? Lists use memory.

Example 4-2 shows how a generator function would dole out the lines.

Example 4-2. Use `yield`

```
>>> def doh2():
...     yield "Homer: D'oh!"
...     yield "Marge: A deer!"
...     yield "Lisa: A female deer!"
...
>>> for line in doh2():
...     print(line)
...
Homer: D'oh!
```

```
Marge: A deer!
Lisa: A female deer!
```

Instead of iterating over a list returned by the plain function doh(), we're iterating over a *generator object* returned by the *generator function* doh2(). The actual iteration (for...in) looks the same. Python returns the first string from doh2(), but keeps track of where it is for the next iteration, and so on until the function runs out of dialogue.

Any function containing yield is a generator function. Given this ability to go back into the middle of a function and resume execution, the next section looks like a logical adaptation.

Python async, await, and asyncio

Python's asyncio (*https://oreil.ly/cBMAc*) features have been introduced over various releases. You're running at least Python 3.7, when the async and await terms became reserved keywords.

The following examples show a joke that's funny only when run asynchronously. Run both yourself, because the timing matters.

First, run the unfunny Example 4-3.

Example 4-3. Dullness

```
>>> import time
>>>
>>> def q():
...     print("Why can't programmers tell jokes?")
...     time.sleep(3)
...
>>> def a():
...     print("Timing!")
...
>>> def main():
...     q()
...     a()
...
>>> main()
Why can't programmers tell jokes?
Timing!
```

You'll see a three-second gap between the question and answer. Yawn.

But the async Example 4-4 is a little different.

Example 4-4. Hilarity

```
>>> import asyncio
>>>
>>> async def q():
...     print("Why can't programmers tell jokes?")
...     await asyncio.sleep(3)
...
>>> async def a():
...     print("Timing!")
...
>>> async def main():
...     await asyncio.gather(q(), a())
...
>>> asyncio.run(main())
Why can't programmers tell jokes?
Timing!
```

This time, the answer should pop out right after the question, followed by three seconds of silence—just as though a programmer is telling it. Ha ha! Ahem.

 I've used `asyncio.gather()` and `asyncio.run()` in Example 4-4, but there are multiple ways of calling async functions. When using FastAPI, you won't need to use these.

Python thinks this when running Example 4-4:

1. Execute q(). Well, just the first line right now.

2. OK, you lazy async q(), I've set my stopwatch and I'll come back to you in three seconds.

3. In the meantime I'll run a(), printing the answer right away.

4. No other await, so back to q().

5. Boring event loop! I'll sit here aaaand stare for the rest of the three seconds.

6. OK, now I'm done.

This example uses `asyncio.sleep()` for a function that takes some time, much like a function that reads a file or accesses a website. You put await in front of the function that might spend most of its time waiting. And that function needs to have async before its def.

If you define a function with `async def`, its caller must put an `await` before the call to it. And the caller itself must be declared `async def`, and *its* caller must `await` it, all the way up.

By the way, you can declare a function as `async` even if it doesn't contain an `await` call to another async function. It doesn't hurt.

FastAPI and Async

After that long field trip over hill and dale, let's get back to FastAPI and why any of it matters.

Because web servers spend a lot of time waiting, performance can be increased by avoiding some of that waiting—in other words, concurrency. Other web servers use many of the methods mentioned earlier: threads, gevent, and so on. One of the reasons that FastAPI is one of the fastest Python web frameworks is its incorporation of async code, via the underlying Starlette package's ASGI support, and some of its own inventions.

The use of `async` and `await` on their own does not make code run faster. In fact, it might be a little slower, from async setup overhead. The main use of `async` is to avoid long waits for I/O.

Now, let's look at our earlier web endpoint calls and see how to make them async.

The functions that map URLs to code are called *path functions* in the FastAPI docs. I've also called them *web endpoints*, and you saw synchronous examples of them in Chapter 3. Let's make some async ones. As in those earlier examples, we'll just use simple types like numbers and strings for now. Chapter 5 introduces *type hints* and Pydantic, which we'll need to handle fancier data structures.

Example 4-5 revisits the first FastAPI program from the previous chapter and makes it asynchronous.

Example 4-5. A shy async endpoint (greet_async.py)

```
from fastapi import FastAPI
import asyncio

app = FastAPI()

@app.get("/hi")
async def greet():
    await asyncio.sleep(1)
    return "Hello? World?"
```

To run that chunk of web code, you need a web server like Uvicorn.

The first way is to run Uvicorn on the command line:

```
$ uvicorn greet_async:app
```

The second, as in Example 4-6, is to call Uvicorn from inside the example code, when it's run as a main program instead of a module.

Example 4-6. Another shy async endpoint (greet_async_uvicorn.py)

```
from fastapi import FastAPI
import asyncio
import uvicorn

app = FastAPI()

@app.get("/hi")
async def greet():
    await asyncio.sleep(1)
    return "Hello? World?"

if __name__ == "__main__":
    uvicorn.run("greet_async_uvicorn:app")
```

When run as a standalone program, Python names it main. That if __name__ ... stuff is Python's way of running it only when called as a main program. Yes, it's ugly.

This code will pause for one second before returning its timorous greeting. The only difference from a synchronous function that used the standard sleep(1) function is that the web server can handle other requests in the meantime with the async example.

Using asyncio.sleep(1) fakes a real-world function that might take one second, like calling a database or downloading a web page. Later chapters will show examples of such calls from this Web layer to the Service layer, and from there to the Data layer, actually spending that wait time on real work.

FastAPI calls this async greet() path function itself when it receives a GET request for the URL /hi. You don't need to add an await anywhere. But for any other async def function definitions that you make, the caller must put an await before each call.

 FastAPI runs an async *event loop* that coordinates the async path functions, and a *threadpool* for synchronous path functions. A developer doesn't need to know the tricky details, which is a great plus. For example, you don't need to run methods like asyncio.gather() or asyncio.run(), as in the (standalone, non-FastAPI) joke example earlier.

Using Starlette Directly

FastAPI doesn't expose Starlette as much as it does Pydantic. Starlette is largely the machinery humming in the engine room, keeping the ship running smoothly.

But if you're curious, you could use Starlette directly to write a web application. Example 3-1 in the previous chapter might look like Example 4-7.

Example 4-7. Using Starlette: starlette_hello.py

```python
from starlette.applications import Starlette
from starlette.responses import JSONResponse
from starlette.routing import Route

async def greeting(request):
    return JSONResponse('Hello? World?')

app = Starlette(debug=True, routes=[
    Route('/hi', greeting),
])
```

Run this web application with this:

```
$ uvicorn starlette_hello:app
```

In my opinion, the FastAPI additions make web API development much easier.

Interlude: Cleaning the Clue House

You own a small (very small: just you) house-cleaning company. You've been living on ramen but just landed a contract that will let you afford much better ramen.

Your client bought an old mansion that was built in the style of the board game Clue and wants to host a character party there soon. But the place is an incredible mess. If Marie Kondo saw the place, she might do the following:

- Scream
- Gag
- Run away
- All of the above

Your contract includes a speed bonus. How can you clean the place thoroughly, in the least amount of elapsed time? The best approach would have been to have more Clue Preservation Units (CPUs), but you're it.

So you can try one of these:

- Do everything in one room, then everything in the next, etc.
- Do a specific task in one room, then the next, etc. Like polishing the silver in the Kitchen and Dining Room, or the pool balls in the Billiard Room.

Would your total time for these approaches differ? Maybe. But it might be more important to consider whether you have to wait an appreciable time for any step. An example might be underfoot: after cleaning rugs and waxing floors, they might need to dry for hours before moving furniture back onto them.

So, here's your plan for each room:

1. Clean all the static parts (windows, etc.).
2. Move all the furniture from the room into the Hall.
3. Remove years of grime from the rug and/or hardwood floor.
4. Do either of these:
   a. Wait for the rug or wax to dry, but wave your bonus goodbye.
   b. Go to the next room now, and repeat. After the last room, move the furniture back into the first room, and so on.

The waiting-to-dry approach is the synchronous one, and it might be best if time isn't a factor and you need a break. The second is async and saves the waiting time for each room.

Let's assume you choose the async path, because money. You get the old dump to sparkle and receive that bonus from your grateful client. The later party turns out to be a great success, except for these issues:

1. One memeless guest came as Mario.
2. You overwaxed the dance floor in the Ball Room, and a tipsy Professor Plum skated about in his socks, until he sailed into a table and spilled champagne on Miss Scarlet.

Morals of this story:

- Requirements can be conflicting and/or strange.
- Estimating time and effort can depend on many factors.
- Sequencing tasks may be as much art as science.
- You'll feel great when it's all done. Mmm, ramen.

Review

After an overview of ways of increasing concurrency, this chapter expanded on functions that use the recent Python keywords `async` and `await`. It showed how FastAPI and Starlette handle both plain old synchronous functions and these new async funky functions.

The next chapter introduces the second leg of FastAPI: how Pydantic helps you define your data.

## CHAPTER 5

Pydantic, Type Hints, and Models Tour

Data validation and settings management using Python type hints.

Fast and extensible, Pydantic plays nicely with your linters/IDE/brain. Define how data should be in pure, canonical Python 3.6+; validate it with Pydantic.

—Samuel Colvin, developer of Pydantic

Preview

FastAPI stands largely on a Python package called Pydantic. This uses *models* (Python object classes) to define data structures. These are heavily used in FastAPI applications and are a real advantage when writing larger applications.

Type Hinting

It's time to learn a little more about Python *type hints*.

Chapter 2 mentioned that, in many computer languages, a variable points directly to a value in memory. This requires the programmer to declare its type, so the size and bits of the value can be determined. In Python, variables are just names associated with objects, and it's the objects that have types.

In standard programming, a variable is usually associated with the same object. If we associate a type hint with that variable, we can avoid some programming mistakes. So Python added type hinting to the language, in the standard typing module. The Python interpreter ignores the type hint syntax and runs the program as though it isn't there. Then what's the point?

You might treat a variable as a string in one line, and forget later and assign it an object of a different type. Although compilers for other languages would complain, Python won't. The standard Python interpreter will catch normal syntax errors and runtime exceptions, but not mixing types for a variable. Helper tools like mypy pay attention to type hints and warn you about any mismatches.

Also, the hints are available to Python developers, who can write tools that do more than type error checking. The following sections describe how the Pydantic package was developed to address needs that weren't obvious. Later, you'll see how its integration with FastAPI makes a lot of web development issues much easier to handle.

By the way, what do type hints look like? There's one syntax for variables and another for function return values.

Variable type hints may include only the type:

```
name: type
```

or also initialize the variable with a value:

```
name: type = value
```

The *type* can be one of the standard Python simple types like int or str, or collection types like tuple, list, or dict:

```
thing: str = "yeti"
```

 Before Python 3.9, you need to import capitalized versions of these standard type names from the typing module:

```
from typing import Str
thing: Str = "yeti"
```

Here are some examples with initializations:

```
physics_magic_number: float = 1.0/137.03599913
hp_lovecraft_noun: str = "ichor"
exploding_sheep: tuple = "sis", "boom", bah!"
responses: dict = {"Marco": "Polo", "answer": 42}
```

You can also include subtypes of collections:

```
name: dict[keytype, valtype] = {key1: val1, key2: val2}
```

The typing module has useful extras for subtypes; the most common are as follows:

Any
    Any type

Union
    Any type of those specified, such as Union[str, int].

In Python 3.10 and up, you can say *type1 | type2* instead of Union[*type1, type2*].

Examples of Pydantic definitions for a Python `dict` include the following:

```
from typing import Any
responses: dict[str, Any] = {"Marco": "Polo", "answer": 42}
```

Or, a little more specific:

```
from typing import Union
responses: dict[str, Union[str, int]] = {"Marco": "Polo", "answer": 42}
```

or (Python 3.10 and up):

```
responses: dict[str, str | int] = {"Marco": "Polo", "answer": 42}
```

Notice that a type-hinted variable line is legal Python, but a bare variable line is not:

```
$ python
...
>>> thing0
Traceback (most recent call last):
  File "<stdin>", line 1, in <module>
NameError: name thing0 is not defined
>>> thing0: str
```

Also, incorrect type uses are not caught by the regular Python interpreter:

```
$ python
...
>>> thing1: str = "yeti"
>>> thing1 = 47
```

But they will be caught by mypy. If you don't already have it, run `pip install mypy`. Save those two preceding lines to a file called *stuff.py*,[1] and then try this:

```
$ mypy stuff.py
stuff.py:2: error: Incompatible types in assignment
(expression has type "int", variable has type "str")
Found 1 error in 1 file (checked 1 source file)
```

A function return type hint uses an arrow instead of a colon:

```
function(args) -> type:
```

---

1 Do I have any detectable imagination? Hmm…no.

Here's a Pydantic example of a function return:

```
def get_thing() -> str:
    return "yeti"
```

You can use any type, including classes that you've defined or combinations of them. You'll see that in a few pages.

Data Grouping

Often we need to keep a related group of variables together rather than passing around lots of individual variables. How do we integrate multiple variables as a group and keep the type hints?

Let's leave behind our tepid greeting example from previous chapters and start using richer data from now on. As in the rest of this book, we'll use examples of *cryptids* (imaginary creatures) and the (also imaginary) explorers who seek them. Our initial cryptid definitions will include only string variables for the following:

name
> Key

country
> Two-character ISO country code (3166-1 alpha 2) or * = all

area
> Optional; United States state or other country subdivision

description
> Free-form

aka
> Also known as…

And explorers will have the following:

name
> Key

country
> Two-character ISO country code

description
> Free-form

Python's historic data grouping structures (beyond the basic `int`, `string`, and such) are listed here:

`tuple`
> An immutable sequence of objects

`list`
> A mutable sequence of objects

`set`
> Mutable distinct objects

`dict`
> Mutable key-value object pairs (the key needs to be of an immutable type)

Tuples (Example 5-1) and lists (Example 5-2) let you access a member variable only by its offset, so you have to remember what went where.

Example 5-1. Using a tuple

```
>>> tuple_thing = ("yeti", "CN", "Himalayas",
    "Hirsute Himalayan", "Abominable Snowman")
>>> print("Name is", tuple_thing[0])
Name is yeti
```

Example 5-2. Using a list

```
>>> list_thing = ["yeti", "CN", "Himalayas",
    "Hirsute Himalayan", "Abominable Snowman"]
>>> print("Name is", list_thing[0])
Name is yeti
```

Example 5-3 shows that you can get a little more explanatory by defining names for the integer offsets.

Example 5-3. Using tuples and named offsets

```
>>> NAME = 0
>>> COUNTRY = 1
>>> AREA = 2
>>> DESCRIPTION = 3
>>> AKA = 4
>>> tuple_thing = ("yeti", "CN", "Himalayas",
    "Hirsute Himalayan", "Abominable Snowman")
>>> print("Name is", tuple_thing[NAME])
Name is yeti
```

Dictionaries are a little better in Example 5-4, giving you access by descriptive keys.

Example 5-4. Using a dictionary

```
>>> dict_thing = {"name": "yeti",
...     "country": "CN",
...     "area": "Himalayas",
...     "description": "Hirsute Himalayan",
...     "aka": "Abominable Snowman"}
>>> print("Name is", dict_thing["name"])
Name is yeti
```

Sets contain only unique values, so they're not very helpful for clustering various variables.

In Example 5-5, a *named tuple* is a tuple that gives you access by integer offset *or* name.

Example 5-5. Using a named tuple

```
>>> from collections import namedtuple
>>> CreatureNamedTuple = namedtuple("CreatureNamedTuple",
...     "name, country, area, description, aka")
>>> namedtuple_thing = CreatureNamedTuple("yeti",
...     "CN",
...     "Himalaya",
...     "Hirsute HImalayan",
...     "Abominable Snowman")
>>> print("Name is", namedtuple_thing[0])
Name is yeti
>>> print("Name is", namedtuple_thing.name)
Name is yeti
```

> You can't say namedtuple_thing["name"]. It's a tuple, not a dict, so the index needs to be an integer.

Example 5-6 defines a new Python class and adds all the attributes with self. But you'll need to do a lot of typing just to define them.

Example 5-6. Using a standard class

```
>>> class CreatureClass():
...     def __init__(self,
...         name: str,
...         country: str,
...         area: str,
...         description: str,
...         aka: str):
```

```
...         self.name = name
...         self.country = country
...         self.area = area
...         self.description = description
...         self.aka = aka
...
>>> class_thing = CreatureClass(
...     "yeti",
...     "CN",
...     "Himalayas"
...     "Hirsute Himalayan",
...     "Abominable Snowman")
>>> print("Name is", class_thing.name)
Name is yeti
```

 You might think, what's so bad about that? With a regular class, you can add more data (attributes), but especially behavior (methods). You might decide, one madcap day, to add a method that looks up an explorer's favorite songs. (This wouldn't apply to a creature.[2]) But the use case here is just to move a clump of data undisturbed among the layers, and to validate on the way in and out. Also, methods are square pegs that would struggle to fit in the round holes of a database.

Does Python have anything similar to what other computer languages call a *record* or a *struct* (a group of names and values)? A recent addition to Python is the *dataclass*. Example 5-7 shows how all that `self` stuff disappears with dataclasses.

Example 5-7. Using a dataclass

```
>>> from dataclasses import dataclass
>>>
>>> @dataclass
... class CreatureDataClass():
...     name: str
...     country: str
...     area: str
...     description: str
...     aka: str
...
>>> dataclass_thing = CreatureDataClass(
...     "yeti",
...     "CN",
...     "Himalayas"
...     "Hirsute Himalayan",
```

---

2 Except that small group of yodeling yetis (a good name for a band).

```
...      "Abominable Snowman")
>>> print("Name is", dataclass_thing.name)
Name is yeti
```

This is pretty good for the keeping-variables-together part. But we want more, so let's ask Santa for these:

- A *union* of possible alternative types
- Missing/optional values
- Default values
- Data validation
- Serialization to and from formats like JSON

Alternatives

It's tempting to use Python's built-in data structures, especially dictionaries. But you'll inevitably find that dictionaries are a bit too "loose." Freedom comes at a price. You need to check *everything*:

- Is the key optional?
- If the key is missing, is there a default value?
- Does the key exist?
- If so, is the key's value of the right type?
- If so, is the value in the right range or matching a pattern?

At least three solutions address at least some of these requirements:

Dataclasses (https://oreil.ly/mxANA)
    Part of standard Python.

attrs (https://www.attrs.org)
    Third party, but a superset of dataclasses.

Pydantic (https://docs.pydantic.dev)
    Also third party, but integrated into FastAPI, so an easy choice if you're already using FastAPI. And if you're reading this book, that's likely.

A handy comparison of the three is on YouTube (*https://oreil.ly/pkQD3*). One take-away is that Pydantic stands out for validation, and its integration with FastAPI catches many potential data errors. Another is that Pydantic relies on inheritance (from the `BaseModel` class), and the other two use Python decorators to define their objects. This is more a matter of style.

In another comparison (*https://oreil.ly/gU28a*), Pydantic outperformed older validation packages like marshmallow (*https://marshmallow.readthedocs.io*) and the intriguingly named Voluptuous (*https://github.com/alecthomas/voluptuous*). Another big plus for Pydantic is that it uses standard Python type hint syntax; older libraries predated type hints and rolled their own.

So I'm going with Pydantic in this book, but you may find uses for either of the alternatives if you're not using FastAPI.

Pydantic provides ways to specify any combination of these checks:

- Required versus optional
- Default value if unspecified but required
- The data type or types expected
- Value range restrictions
- Other function-based checks if needed
- Serialization and deserialization

A Simple Example

You've seen how to feed a simple string to a web endpoint via the URL, a query parameter, or the HTTP body. The problem is that you usually request and receive groups of data, of many types. That's where Pydantic models first appear in FastAPI.

This initial example will use three files:

- *model.py* defines a Pydantic model.
- *data.py* is a fake data source, defining an instance of a model.
- *web.py* defines a FastAPI web endpoint that returns the fake data.

For simplicity in this chapter, let's keep all the files in the same directory. In later chapters that discuss larger websites, we'll separate them into their respective layers. First, define the *model* for a creature in Example 5-8.

Example 5-8. Define a creature model: model.py

```
from pydantic import BaseModel

class Creature(BaseModel):
    name: str
    country: str
    area: str
    description: str
    aka: str
```

```
thing = Creature(
    name="yeti",
    country="CN",
    area="Himalayas",
    description="Hirsute Himalayan",
    aka="Abominable Snowman")
)
print("Name is", thing.name)
```

The Creature class inherits from Pydantic's BaseModel. That : str part after name, country, area, description, and aka is a type hint that each is a Python string.

 In this example, all fields are required. In Pydantic, if Optional is not in the type description, the field must have a value.

In Example 5-9, pass the arguments in any order if you include their names.

Example 5-9. Create a creature

```
>>> thing = Creature(
...     name="yeti",
...     country="CN",
...     area="Himalayas"
...     description="Hirsute Himalayan",
...     aka="Abominable Snowman")
>>> print("Name is", thing.name)
Name is yeti
```

For now, Example 5-10 defines a teeny source of data; in later chapters, databases will do this. The type hint list[Creature] tells Python that this is a list of Creature objects only.

Example 5-10. Define fake data in data.py

```
from model import Creature

_creatures: list[Creature] = [
    Creature(name="yeti",
            country="CN",
            area="Himalayas",
            description="Hirsute Himalayan",
            aka="Abominable Snowman"
            ),
    Creature(name="sasquatch",
            country="US",
```

```
        area="*",
        description="Yeti's Cousin Eddie",
        aka="Bigfoot")
]

def get_creatures() -> list[Creature]:
    return _creatures
```

(We're using "*" for Bigfoot's area because he's almost everywhere.)

This code imports the *model.py* that we just wrote. It does a little data hiding by calling its list of Creature objects _creatures, and providing the get_creatures() function to return them.

Example 5-11 lists *web.py*, a file that defines a FastAPI web endpoint.

Example 5-11. Define a FastAPI web endpoint: web.py

```
from model import Creature
from fastapi import FastAPI

app = FastAPI()

@app.get("/creature")
def get_all() -> list[Creature]:
    from data import get_creatures
    return get_creatures()
```

Now fire up this one-endpoint server in Example 5-12.

Example 5-12. Start Uvicorn

```
$ uvicorn creature:app
INFO:     Started server process [24782]
INFO:     Waiting for application startup.
INFO:     Application startup complete.
INFO:     Uvicorn running on http://127.0.0.1:8000 (Press CTRL+C to quit)
```

In another window, Example 5-13 accesses the web application with the HTTPie web client (try your browser or the Requests module if you like too).

Example 5-13. Test with HTTPie

```
$ http http://localhost:8000/creature
HTTP/1.1 200 OK
content-length: 183
content-type: application/json
date: Mon, 12 Sep 2022 02:21:15 GMT
server: uvicorn
```

```
[
    {
        "aka": "Abominable Snowman",
        "area": "Himalayas",
        "country": "CN",
        "name": "yeti",
        "description": "Hirsute Himalayan"
    },
    {
        "aka": "Bigfoot",
        "country": "US",
        "area": "*",
        "name": "sasquatch",
        "description": "Yeti's Cousin Eddie"
    }
}
```

FastAPI and Starlette automatically convert the original Creature model object list into a JSON string. This is the default output format in FastAPI, so we don't need to specify it.

Also, the window in which you originally started the Uvicorn web server should have printed a log line:

```
INFO:     127.0.0.1:52375 - "GET /creature HTTP/1.1" 200 OK
```

Validate Types

The previous section showed how to do the following:

- Apply type hints to variables and functions
- Define and use a Pydantic model
- Return a list of models from a data source
- Return the model list to a web client, automatically converting the model list to JSON

Now, let's really put it to work validating data.

Try assigning a value of the wrong type to one or more of the Creature fields. Let's use a standalone test for this (Pydantic doesn't apply on any web code; it's a data thing).

Example 5-14 lists *test1.py*.

Example 5-14. Test the Creature model

```
from model import Creature

dragon = Creature(
    name="dragon",
    description=["incorrect", "string", "list"],
    country="*" ,
    area="*",
    aka="firedrake")
```

Now try the test in Example 5-15.

Example 5-15. Run the test

```
$ python test1.py
Traceback (most recent call last):
  File ".../test1.py", line 3, in <module>
    dragon = Creature(
  File "pydantic/main.py", line 342, in
    pydantic.main.BaseModel.init
    pydantic.error_wrappers.ValidationError:
    1 validation error for Creature description
  str type expected (type=type_error.str)
```

This finds that we've assigned a list of strings to the description field, and it wants a plain old string.

Validate Values

Even if the value's type matches its specification in the Creature class, more checks may need to pass. Some restrictions can be placed on the value itself:

- Integer (conint) or float:

  gt
    Greater than

  lt
    Less than

  ge
    Greater than or equal to

  le
    Less than or equal to

multiple_of
> An integer multiple of a value

- String (constr):

min_length
> Minimum character (not byte) length

max_length
> Maximum character length

to_upper
> Convert to uppercase

to_lower
> Convert to lowercase

regex
> Match a Python regular expression

- Tuple, list, or set:

min_items
> Minimum number of elements

max_items
> Maximum number of elements

These are specified in the type parts of the model.

Example 5-16 ensures that the name field is always at least two characters long. Otherwise, "" (an empty string) is a valid string.

Example 5-16. See a validation failure

```
>>> from pydantic import BaseModel, constr
>>>
>>> class Creature(BaseModel):
...     name: constr(min_length=2)
...     country: str
...     area: str
...     description: str
...     aka: str
...
>>> bad_creature = Creature(name="!",
...     description="it's a raccoon",
...     area="your attic")
Traceback (most recent call last):
  File "<stdin>", line 1, in <module>
```

```
  File "pydantic/main.py", line 342,
  in pydantic.main.BaseModel.__init__
pydantic.error_wrappers.ValidationError:
1 validation error for Creature name
  ensure this value has at least 2 characters
  (type=value_error.any_str.min_length; limit_value=2)
```

That `constr` means a *constrained string*. Example 5-17 uses an alternative, the Pydantic `Field` specification.

Example 5-17. Another validation failure, using `Field`

```
>>> from pydantic import BaseModel, Field
>>>
>>> class Creature(BaseModel):
...     name: str = Field(..., min_length=2)
...     country: str
...     area: str
...     description: str
...     aka: str
...
>>> bad_creature = Creature(name="!",
...     area="your attic",
...     description="it's a raccoon")
Traceback (most recent call last):
  File "<stdin>", line 1, in <module>
  File "pydantic/main.py", line 342,
  in pydantic.main.BaseModel.__init__
pydantic.error_wrappers.ValidationError:
1 validation error for Creature name
  ensure this value has at least 2 characters
  (type=value_error.any_str.min_length; limit_value=2)
```

That `...` argument to `Field()` means that a value is required, and that there's no default value.

This is a minimal introduction to Pydantic. The main takeaway is that it lets you automate the validation of your data. You'll see how useful this is when getting data from either the Web or Data layers.

Review

Models are the best way to define data that will be passed around in your web application. Pydantic leverages Python's *type hints* to define data models to pass around in your application. Coming next: defining *dependencies* to separate specific details from your general code.

## CHAPTER 6

Dependencies

Preview

One of the very nice design features of FastAPI is a technique called *dependency injection*. This term sounds technical and esoteric, but it's a key aspect of FastAPI and is surprisingly useful at many levels. This chapter looks at FastAPI's built-in capabilities as well as how to write your own.

What's a Dependency?

A *dependency* is specific information that you need at some point. The usual way to get this information is to write code that gets it, right when you need it.

When you're writing a web service, at some time you may need to do the following:

- Gather input parameters from the HTTP request
- Validate inputs
- Check user authentication and authorization for some endpoints
- Look up data from a data source, often a database
- Emit metrics, logs, or tracking information

Web frameworks convert the HTTP request bytes to data structures, and you pluck what you need from them inside your Web layer functions as you go.

Problems with Dependencies

Getting what you want, right when you need it, and without external code needing to know how you got it, seems pretty reasonable. But it turns out that consequences exist:

Testing
> You can't test variations of your function that could look up the dependency differently.

Hidden dependencies
> Hiding the details means that code your function needs could break when external code changes.

Code duplication
> If your dependency is a common one (like looking up a user in a database or combining values from an HTTP request), you might duplicate the lookup code in multiple functions.

OpenAPI visibility
> The automatic test page that FastAPI makes for you needs information from the dependency injection mechanism.

Dependency Injection

The term *dependency injection* is simpler than it sounds: pass any *specific* information that a function needs *into* the function. A traditional way to do this is to pass in a helper function, which you then call to get the specific data.

FastAPI Dependencies

FastAPI goes one step more: you can define dependencies as arguments to your function, and they are *automatically* called by FastAPI and pass in the *values* that they return. For example, a `user_dep` dependency could get the user's name and password from HTTP arguments, look them up in a database, and return a token that you use to track that user afterward. Your web-handling function doesn't ever call this directly; it's handled at function call time.

You've already seen some dependencies but didn't see them referred to as such: HTTP data sources like `Path`, `Query`, `Body`, and `Header`. These are functions or Python classes that dig the requested data from various areas in the HTTP request. They hide the details, like validity checks and data formats.

Why not write your own functions to do this? You could, but you would not have these:

- Data validity checks
- Format conversions
- Automatic documentation

In many other web frameworks, you would do these checks inside your own functions. You'll see examples of this in Chapter 7, which compares FastAPI with Python web frameworks like Flask and Django. But in FastAPI, you can handle your own dependencies, much as the built-in ones do.

Writing a Dependency

In FastAPI, a dependency is something that's executed, so a dependency object needs to be of the type `Callable`, which includes functions and classes—things that you *call*, with parentheses and optional arguments.

Example 6-1 shows a `user_dep()` dependency function that takes name and password string arguments, and just returns `True` if the user is valid. For this first version, let's have the function return `True` for anything.

Example 6-1. A dependency function

```
from fastapi import FastAPI, Depends, Params

app = FastAPI()

# the dependency function:
def user_dep(name: str = Params, password: str = Params):
    return {"name": name, "valid": True}

# the path function / web endpoint:
@app.get("/user")
def get_user(user: dict = Depends(user_dep)) -> dict:
    return user
```

Here, `user_dep()` is a dependency function. It acts like a FastAPI path function (it knows about things like `Params`, etc.), but doesn't have a path decorator above it. It's a helper, not a web endpoint itself.

The path function `get_user()` says that it expects an argument variable called `user`, and that variable will get its value from the dependency function `user_dep()`.

In the arguments to get_user(), we could not have said user = user_dep, because user_dep is a Python function object. And we could not say user = user_dep(), because that would have called the user_dep() function when get_user() was *defined*, not when it's used. So we need that extra helper FastAPI Depends() function to call user_dep() just when it's wanted.

You can have multiple dependencies in your path function argument list.

Dependency Scope

You can define dependencies to cover a single path function, a group of them, or the whole web application.

Single Path

In your *path function*, include an argument like this:

```
def pathfunc(name: depfunc = Depends(depfunc)):
```

or just this:

```
def pathfunc(name: depfunc = Depends()):
```

name is whatever you want to call the value(s) returned by *depfunc*.

From the earlier example:

- *pathfunc* is get_user().
- *depfunc* is user_dep().
- *name* is user.

Example 6-2 uses this path and dependency to return a fixed user name and a valid Boolean.

Example 6-2. Return a user dependency

```
from fastapi import FastAPI, Depends, Params

app = FastAPI()

# the dependency function:
def user_dep(name: str = Params, password: str = Params):
    return {"name": name, "valid": True}

# the path function / web endpoint:
@app.get("/user")
```

```
def get_user(user: dict = Depends(user_dep)) -> dict:
    return user
```

If your dependency function just checks something and doesn't return any values, you can also define the dependency in your path *decorator* (the preceding line, starting with a @):

```
@app.method(url, dependencies=[Depends(depfunc)])
```

Let's try that in Example 6-3.

Example 6-3. Define a user check dependency

```
from fastapi import FastAPI, Depends, Params

app = FastAPI()

# the dependency function:
def check_dep(name: str = Params, password: str = Params):
    if not name:
        raise

# the path function / web endpoint:
@app.get("/check_user", dependencies=[Depends(check_dep)])
def check_user() -> bool:
    return True
```

Multiple Paths

Chapter 9 gives more details on how to structure a larger FastAPI application, including defining more than one *router* object under a top-level application, instead of attaching every endpoint to the top-level application. Example 6-4 sketches the idea.

Example 6-4. Define a subrouter dependency

```
from fastapi import FastAPI, Depends, APIRouter

router = APIRouter(..., dependencies=[Depends(depfunc)])
```

This will cause *depfunc()* to be called for all path functions under `router`.

Global

When you define your top-level FastAPI application object, you can add dependencies to it that will apply to all its path functions, as shown in Example 6-5.

Example 6-5. Define app-level dependencies

```
from fastapi import FastAPI, Depends

def depfunc1():
    pass

def depfunc2():
    pass

app = FastAPI(dependencies=[Depends(depfunc1), Depends(depfunc2)])

@app.get("/main")
def get_main():
    pass
```

In this case, you're using pass to ignore the other details to show how to attach the dependencies.

Review

This chapter discussed dependencies and dependency injection—ways of getting the data you need when you need it, in a straightforward way. Coming up in the next chapter: Flask, Django, and FastAPI walk into a bar...

## CHAPTER 7

Framework Comparisons

You don't need a framework. You need a painting, not a frame.

—Klaus Kinski, actor

Preview

For developers who have used Flask, Django, or popular Python web frameworks, this chapter points out FastAPI's similarities and differences. It does not go into every excruciating detail, because, otherwise, the binding glue wouldn't hold this book together. This chapter's comparisons can be useful if you're thinking of migrating an application from one of these frameworks to FastAPI or are just curious.

One of the first things you might like to know about a new web framework is how to get started, and a top-down way is by defining *routes* (mappings from URLs and HTTP methods to functions). The next section compares how to do this with FastAPI and Flask, because they're more similar to one another than Django and are more likely to be considered together for similar applications.

Flask

Flask (*https://flask.palletsprojects.com*) calls itself a *microframework*. It provides the basics, and you download third-party packages to supplement it as needed. It's smaller than Django, and faster to learn when you're getting started.

Flask is synchronous, based on WSGI rather than ASGI. A new project called quart (*https://quart.palletsprojects.com*) is replicating Flask and adding ASGI support.

Let's start at the top, showing how Flask and FastAPI define web routing.

Path

At the top level, Flask and FastAPI both use a decorator to associate a route with a web endpoint. In Example 7-1, let's duplicate Example 3-11 (from back in Chapter 3), which gets the person to greet from the URL path.

Example 7-1. FastAPI path

```
from fastapi import FastAPI

app = FastAPI()

@app.get("/hi/{who}")
def greet(who: str):
    return f"Hello? {who}?"
```

By default, FastAPI converts that f"Hello? {who}?" string to JSON and returns it to the web client.

Example 7-2 shows how Flask would do it.

Example 7-2. Flask path

```
from flask import Flask, jsonify

app = Flask(__name__)

@app.route("/hi/<who>", methods=["GET"])
def greet(who: str):
    return jsonify(f"Hello? {who}?")
```

Notice that the who in the decorator is now bounded by < and >. In Flask, the method needs to be included as an argument—unless it's the default, GET. So methods= ["GET"] could have been omitted here, but being explicit never hurts.

> Flask 2.0 supports the FastAPI-style decorators like @app.get instead of app.route.

The Flask jsonify() function converts its argument to a JSON string and returns it, along with the HTTP response header indicating that it's JSON. If you're returning a dict (not other data types), recent versions of Flask will automatically convert it to JSON and return it. Calling jsonify() explicitly works for all data types, including dict.

Query Parameter

In Example 7-3, let's repeat Example 3-15, where who is passed as a query parameter (after the ? in the URL).

Example 7-3. FastAPI query parameter

```
from fastapi import FastAPI

app = FastAPI()

@app.get("/hi")
def greet(who):
    return f"Hello? {who}?"
```

The Flask equivalent is shown in Example 7-4.

Example 7-4. Flask query parameter

```
from flask import Flask, request, jsonify

app = Flask(__name__)

@app.route("/hi", methods=["GET"])
def greet():
    who: str = request.args.get("who")
    return jsonify(f"Hello? {who}?")
```

In Flask, we need to get request values from the request object. In this case, args is a dict containing the query parameters.

Body

In Example 7-5, let's copy old Example 3-21.

Example 7-5. FastAPI body

```
from fastapi import FastAPI

app = FastAPI()

@app.get("/hi")
def greet(who):
    return f"Hello? {who}?"
```

A Flask version looks like Example 7-6.

Example 7-6. Flask body

```
from flask import Flask, request, jsonify

app = Flask(__name__)

@app.route("/hi", methods=["GET"])
def greet():
    who: str = request.json["who"]
    return jsonify(f"Hello? {who}?")
```

Flask stores JSON input in *request.json*.

Header

Finally, let's repeat Example 3-24 in Example 7-7.

Example 7-7. FastAPI header

```
from fastapi import FastAPI, Header

app = FastAPI()

@app.get("/hi")
def greet(who:str = Header()):
    return f"Hello? {who}?"
```

The Flask version is shown in Example 7-8.

Example 7-8. Flask header

```
from flask import Flask, request, jsonify

app = Flask(__name__)

@app.route("/hi", methods=["GET"])
def greet():
    who: str = request.headers.get("who")
    return jsonify(f"Hello? {who}?")
```

As with query parameters, Flask keeps request data in the `request` object. This time, it's the `headers` `dict` attribute. The header keys are supposed to be case-insensitive.

Django

Django (*https://www.djangoproject.com*) is bigger and more complex than Flask or FastAPI, targeting "perfectionists with deadlines," according to its website. Its built-in object-relational mapper (ORM) is useful for sites with major database backends. It's more of a monolith than a toolkit. Whether the extra complexity and learning curve are justified depends on your application.

Although Django was a traditional WSGI application, version 3.0 added support for ASGI.

Unlike Flask and FastAPI, Django likes to define routes (associating URLs with web functions, which it calls *view functions*) in a single URLConf table, rather than using decorators. This makes it easier to see all your routes in one place, but makes it harder to see what URL is associated with a function when you're looking at just the function.

Other Web Framework Features

In the previous sections comparing the three frameworks, I've mainly compared how to define routes. A web framework might be expected to help in these other areas too:

Forms
All three packages support standard HTML forms.

Files
All these packages handle file uploads and downloads, including multipart HTTP requests and responses.

Templates
A *template language* lets you mix text and code, and is useful for a *content-oriented* website (HTML text with dynamically inserted data), rather than an API website. The best-known Python template package is Jinja (*https://jinja.palletspro jects.com*), and it's supported by Flask, Django, and FastAPI. Django also has its own template language (*https://oreil.ly/OIbVJ*).

If you want to use networking methods beyond basic HTTP, try these:

Server-sent events
Push data to a client as needed. Supported by FastAPI (sse-starlette (*https://oreil.ly/Hv-QP*)), Flask (Flask-SSE (*https://oreil.ly/oz518*)), and Django (Django EventStream (*https://oreil.ly/NlBE5*)).

Queues
Job queues, publish-subscribe, and other networking patterns are supported by external packages like ZeroMQ, Celery, Redis, and RabbitMQ.

WebSockets
Supported by FastAPI (directly), Django (Django Channels (*https://channels.read thedocs.io*)), and Flask (third-party packages).

Databases

Flask and FastAPI do not include any database handling in their base packages, but database handling is a key feature of Django.

Your site's Data layer might access a database at different levels:

- Direct SQL (PostgreSQL, SQLite)
- Direct NoSQL (Redis, MongoDB, Elasticsearch)
- An *ORM* that generates SQL
- An object document/data mapper/manager (ODM) that generates NoSQL

For relational databases, SQLAlchemy (*https://www.sqlalchemy.org*) is an excellent package that includes multiple access levels, from direct SQL up to an ORM. This is a common choice for Flask and FastAPI developers. The author of FastAPI has leveraged both SQLAlchemy and Pydantic for the SQLModel package (*https://sqlmodel.tiangolo.com*), which is discussed more in Chapter 14.

Django is often the framework choice for a site with heavy database needs. It has its own ORM (*https://oreil.ly/eFzZn*) and an automated database admin page (*https://oreil.ly/_al42*). Although some sources recommend letting nontechnical staff use this admin page for routine data management, be careful. In one case, I've seen a nonexpert misunderstand an admin page warning message, resulting in the database needing to be manually restored from a backup.

Chapter 14 discusses FastAPI and databases in more depth.

Recommendations

For API-based services, FastAPI seems to be the best choice now. Flask and FastAPI are about equal in terms of getting a service up and running quickly. Django takes more time to understand but provides many features of use for larger sites, especially those with heavy database reliance.

Other Python Web Frameworks

The current big three Python web frameworks are Flask, Django, and FastAPI. Google `python web frameworks` and you'll get a wealth of suggestions, which I won't repeat here. A few that might not stand out in those lists but that are interesting for one reason or another include the following:

Bottle (https://bottlepy.org/docs/dev)
    A *very* minimal (single Python file) package, good for a quick proof of concept

---

Litestar (https://litestar.dev)
> Similar to FastAPI—it's based on ASGI/Starlette and Pydantic—but has its own opinions

AIOHTTP (https://docs.aiohttp.org)
> An ASGI client and server, with useful demo code

Socketify.py (https://docs.socketify.dev)
> A new entrant that claims very high performance

Review

Flask and Django are the most popular Python web frameworks, although FastAPI's popularity is growing faster. All three handle the basic web server tasks, with varying learning curves. FastAPI seems to have a cleaner syntax for specifying routes, and its support of ASGI allows it to run faster than its competitors in many cases. Coming next: let's build a website already.

## PART III

Making a Website

Part II was a quick tour of FastAPI, to get you up to speed quickly. This part will go wider and deeper into the details. We'll build a medium-sized web service to access and manage data about cryptids—imaginary creatures—and the equally fictitious explorers who seek them.

The full service will have three layers, as I've discussed earlier:

Web
> The web interface

Service
> The business logic

Data
> The precious DNA of the whole thing

Plus the web service will have these cross-layer components:

Model
> Pydantic data definitions

Tests
> Unit, integration, and end-to-end tests

The site design will address the following:

- What belongs inside each layer?
- What is passed between layers?
- Can we change/add/delete code later without breaking anything?
- If something breaks, how do I find and fix it?
- What about security?
- Can the site scale and perform well?
- Can we keep all this as clear and simple as possible?
- Why do I ask so many questions? Why, oh why?

## CHAPTER 8

Web Layer

Preview

Chapter 3 was a quick look at how to define FastAPI web endpoints, pass simple string inputs to them, and get responses. This chapter goes further into the top layer of a FastAPI application—which could also be called an *Interface* or *Router* layer—and its integration with the Service and Data layers.

As before, I'll start with small examples. Then I'll introduce some structure, dividing layers into subsections to allow for cleaner development and growth. The less code we write, the less we'll need to remember and fix later.

The basic sample data in this book concerns imaginary creatures, or *cryptids*, and their explorers. You may find parallels with other domains of information.

What do we do with information, in general? Like most websites, ours will provide ways to do the following:

- Retrieve
- Create
- Modify
- Replace
- Delete

Starting from the top, we'll create web endpoints that perform these functions on our data. At first, we'll provide fake data to make the endpoints work with any web client. In the following chapters, we'll move the fake data code down into the lower layers. At each step, we'll ensure that the site still works and passes data through correctly.

Finally, in Chapter 10, we'll drop the faking and store real data in real databases, for a full end-to-end (Web → Service → Data) website.

 Allowing any anonymous visitor to perform all these actions will be an object lesson in "why we can't have nice things." Chapter 11 discusses the *auth* (authentication and authorization) needed to define roles and limit who can do what. For the rest of the current chapter, we'll sidestep auth and just show how to handle the raw web functions.

Interlude: Top-Down, Bottom-Up, Middle-Out?

When designing a website, you could start from one of the following:

- The Web layer and work down
- The Data layer and work up
- The Service layer and work out in both directions

Do you already have a database, installed and loaded with data, and are just pining for a way to share it with the world? If so, you may want to tackle the Data layer's code and tests first, then the Service layer, and write the Web layer last.

If you're following domain-driven design (*https://oreil.ly/iJu9Q*), you might start in the middle Service layer, defining your core entities and data models. Or you may want to evolve the web interface first, and fake calls to the lower layers until you know what you'll expect of them.

You'll find very good design discussions and recommendations in these books:

- *Clean Architectures in Python* (*https://oreil.ly/5KrL9*) by Leonardo Giordani (Digital Cat Books)
- *Architecture Patterns with Python* (*https://www.cosmicpython.com*) by Harry J.W. Percival and Bob Gregory (O'Reilly)
- *Microservice APIs* (*https://oreil.ly/Gk0z2*) by José Haro Peralta (Manning)

In these and other sources, you'll see terms like *hexagonal architecture*, *ports*, and *adapters*. Your choices on how to proceed largely depend on what data you have already and how you want to approach the work of building a site.

I'm guessing that many of you are mainly interested in trying out FastAPI and its related technologies, and don't necessarily have a predefined mature data domain that you want to instrument right away.

So, in this book I'm taking the web-first approach—step-by-step, starting with essential parts, and adding others as needed on the way down. Sometimes experiments work, sometimes not. I'll avoid the urge to stuff everything into this Web layer at first.

 This Web layer is just one way of passing data between a user and a service. Alternate ways exist, such as by a CLI or software development kit (SDK). In other frameworks, you might see this Web layer called a *view* or *presentation* layer.

RESTful API Design

HTTP is a way to get commands and data between web clients and servers. But, just as you can combine ingredients from your refrigerator in ways from ghastly to gourmet, some recipes for HTTP work better than others.

In Chapter 1, I mentioned that *RESTful* became a useful, though sometimes fuzzy, model for HTTP development. RESTful designs have these core components:

Resources
> The data elements your application manages

IDs
> Unique resource identifiers

URLs
> Structured resource and ID strings

Verbs or actions
> Terms that accompany URLs for different purposes:

> GET
>> Retrieve a resource.

> POST
>> Create a new resource.

> PUT
>> Completely replace a resource.

> PATCH
>> Partially replace a resource.

> DELETE
>> Resource goes kaboom.

You'll see disagreement about the relative merits of PUT versus PATCH. If you don't need to distinguish between a partial modification and a full one (replacement), you may not need both.

General RESTful rules for combining verbs and URLs containing resources and IDs use these patterns of path parameters (content between the / in the URL):

verb /*resource*/
> Apply *verb* to all resources of type *resource*.

verb /*resource*/*id*
> Apply *verb* to the *resource* with ID *id*.

Using the example data for this book, a GET request to the endpoint */thing* would return data on all explorers, but a GET request for */thing/abc* would give you data for only the thing resource with ID abc.

Finally, web requests often carry more information, indicating to do the following:

- Sort results
- Paginate results
- Perform another function

Parameters for these can sometimes be expressed as *path* parameters (tacked onto the end, after another /) but are often included as *query* parameters (*var=val* stuff after the ? in the URL). Because URLs have size limits, large requests are often conveyed in the HTTP body.

Most authors recommend using plurals when naming the resource, and related namespaces like API sections and database tables. I followed this advice for a long time but now feel that singular names are simpler for many reasons (including oddities of the English language):

- Some words are their own plurals: series, fish
- Some words have irregular plurals: children, people
- You need bespoke singular to/from plural conversion code in many places

For these reasons, I'm using a singular naming scheme in many places in this book. This is against usual RESTful advice, so feel free to ignore this if you disagree.

File and Directory Site Layout

Our data mainly concerns creatures and explorers. Initially, we could define all the URLs and their FastAPI path functions for accessing their data in a single Python file. Let's resist that temptation, and start as though we were already a rising star in the cryptid web space. With a good foundation, cool new things are much easier to add.

First, pick a directory on your machine. Name it *fastapi*, or anything that will help you remember where you'll be messing with the code from this book. Within it, create the following subdirectories:

src
> Contains all the website code

> *web*
>> The FastAPI web layer

> *service*
>> The business logic layer

> *data*
>> The storage interface layer

> *model*
>> Pydantic model definitions

> *fake*
>> Early hardwired (*stub*) data

Each of these directories will soon gain three files:

__init__.py
> Needed to treat this directory as a package

creature.py
> Creature code for this layer

explorer.py
> Explorer code for this layer

Many opinions exist on how to lay out sites for development. This design is intended to show the layer separation and leave room for future additions.

Some explanations are needed right now. First, *__init__.py* files are empty. They're sort of a Python hack, so their directory should be treated as a Python *package* that may be imported from. Second, the *fake* directory provides some stub data to higher layers as the lower ones are built.

In addition, Python's *import* logic doesn't work strictly with directory hierarchies. It relies on Python *packages* and *modules*. The *.py* files listed in the tree structure described previously are Python modules (source files). Their parent directories are packages *if* they contain an *__init__.py* file. (This is a convention to tell Python whether, if you have a directory called *sys* and you type `import sys`, you actually want the system one or your local one.)

Python programs can import packages and modules. The Python interpreter has a built-in `sys.path` variable, which includes the location of the standard Python code. The environment variable `PYTHONPATH` is an empty or colon-separated string of directory names that tells Python which parent directories to check before `sys.path` to find the imported modules or packages. So, if you change to your new *fastapi* directory, type this (on Linux or macOS) to ensure that the new code under it will be checked first when importing:

```
$ export PYTHONPATH=$PWD/src
```

That `$PWD` means *print working directory*, and saves you from typing the full path to your *fastapi* directory, although you can if you want. And the `src` part means to look only in there for modules and packages to import.

To set the `PWD` environment variable under Windows, see "Excursus: Setting Environment Variables" at the Python Software Foundation site (*https://oreil.ly/9NRBA*).

Whew.

The First Website Code

This section discusses how to use FastAPI to write requests and responses for a RESTful API site. Then, we'll begin to apply these to our actual, increasingly gnarly, site.

Let's begin with Example 8-1. Within *src*, make this new top-level *main.py* program that will start the Uvicorn program and FastAPI package.

Example 8-1. The main program, main.py

```python
from fastapi import FastAPI


app = FastAPI()


@app.get("/")
def top():
    return "top here"
```

```
if __name__ == "__main__":
    import uvicorn
    uvicorn.run("main:app", reload=True)
```

That `app` is the FastAPI object that ties everything together. Uvicorn's first argument is `"main:app"` because the file is called *main.py*, and the second is `app`, the name of the FastAPI object.

Uvicorn will keep on running, and restart if any code changes in the same directory or any subdirectories. Without `reload=True`, each time you modify your code, you'd need to kill and restart Uvicorn manually. In many of the following examples, you'll just keep changing the same *main.py* file and forcing a restart, instead of creating *main2.py*, *main3.py*, and so on.

Fire up *main.py* in Example 8-2.

Example 8-2. Run the main program

```
$ python main.py &
INFO:      Will watch for changes in these directories: [.../fastapi']
INFO:      Uvicorn running on http://127.0.0.1:8000 (Press CTRL+C to quit)
INFO:      Started reloader process [92543] using StatReload
INFO:      Started server process [92551]
INFO:      Waiting for application startup.
INFO:      Application startup complete.
```

That final `&` puts the program into the background, and you can run other programs in the same terminal window if you like. Or omit the `&` and run your other code in a different window or tab.

Now you can access the site `localhost:8000` with a browser or any of the test programs that you've seen so far. Example 8-3 uses HTTPie:

Example 8-3. Test the main program

```
$ http localhost:8000
HTTP/1.1 200 OK
content-length: 8
content-type: application/json
date: Sun, 05 Feb 2023 03:54:29 GMT
server: uvicorn

"top here"
```

From now on, as you make changes, the web server should restart automatically. If an error kills it, restart it with `python main.py` again.

Example 8-4 adds another test endpoint, using a *path* parameter (part of the URL).

Example 8-4. Add an endpoint

```
import uvicorn
from fastapi import FastAPI

app = FastAPI()

@app.get("/")
def top():
    return "top here"

@app.get("/echo/{thing}")
def echo(thing):
    return f"echoing {thing}"

if __name__ == "__main__":
    uvicorn.run("main:app", reload=True)
```

As soon as you save your changes to *main.py* in your editor, the window where your web server is running should print something like this:

```
WARNING:  StatReload detected changes in 'main.py'. Reloading...
INFO:     Shutting down
INFO:     Waiting for application shutdown.
INFO:     Application shutdown complete.
INFO:     Finished server process [92862]
INFO:     Started server process [92872]
INFO:     Waiting for application startup.
INFO:     Application startup complete.
```

Example 8-5 shows whether the new endpoint was handled correctly (the -b prints only the response body).

Example 8-5. Test new endpoint

```
$ http -b localhost:8000/echo/argh
"echoing argh"
```

In the following sections, we'll add more endpoints to *main.py*.

Requests

An HTTP request consists of a text *header* followed by one or more *body* sections. You could write your own code to parse HTTP into Python data structures, but you wouldn't be the first. In your web application, it's more productive to have these details done for you by a framework.

FastAPI's dependency injection is particularly useful here. Data may come from different parts of the HTTP message, and you've already seen how you can specify one or more of these dependencies to say where the data is located:

Header
    In the HTTP headers

Path
    In the URL

Query
    After the ? in the URL

Body
    In the HTTP body

Other, more indirect, sources include the following:

- Environment variables
- Configuration settings

Example 8-6 features an HTTP request, using our old friend HTTPie, and ignoring the returned HTML body data.

Example 8-6. HTTP request and response headers

```
$ http -p HBh http://example.com/
GET / HTTP/1.1
Accept: /
Accept-Encoding: gzip, deflate
Connection: keep-alive
Host: example.com
User-Agent: HTTPie/3.2.1


HTTP/1.1 200 OK
Age: 374045
Cache-Control: max-age=604800
Content-Encoding: gzip
Content-Length: 648
Content-Type: text/html; charset=UTF-8
Date: Sat, 04 Feb 2023 01:00:21 GMT
Etag: "3147526947+gzip"
Expires: Sat, 11 Feb 2023 01:00:21 GMT
Last-Modified: Thu, 17 Oct 2019 07:18:26 GMT
Server: ECS (cha/80E2)
Vary: Accept-Encoding
X-Cache: HIT
```

The first line asks for the top page at *example.com* (a free website that anyone can use in, well, examples). It asks only for a URL, with no parameters anywhere else. The first block of lines is the HTTP request headers sent to the website, and the next block contains the HTTP response headers.

 Most test examples from here on won't need all those request and response headers, so you'll see more use of http -b.

Multiple Routers

Most web services handle multiple kinds of resources. Although you could throw all your path-handling code in a single file and head off to a happy hour somewhere, it's often handy to use multiple *subrouters* instead of the single app variable that most of the examples up to now have used.

Under the *web* directory (in the same directory as the *main.py* file that you've been modifying so far), make a file called *explorer.py*, as in Example 8-7.

Example 8-7. APIRouter use in web/explorer.py

```
from fastapi import APIRouter

router = APIRouter(prefix = "/explorer")

@router.get("/")
def top():
    return "top explorer endpoint"
```

Now, Example 8-8 gets the top-level application *main.py* to know that there's a new subrouter in town, which will handle all URLs that start with */explorer*:

*Example 8-8. Connect the main application (*main.py*) to the subrouter*

```
from fastapi import FastAPI
from .web import explorer

app = FastAPI()

app.include_router(explorer.router)
```

This new file will be picked up by Uvicorn. As usual, test in Example 8-9 instead of assuming it will work.

Example 8-9. Test new subrouter

```
$ http -b localhost:8000/explorer/
"top explorer endpoint"
```

Build the Web Layer

Now let's start adding the actual core functions to the Web layer. Initially, fake all the data in the web functions themselves. In Chapter 9, we will move the fake data stuff to corresponding service functions, and in Chapter 10, to the data functions. Finally, an actual database will be added for the Data layer to access. At each development step, calls to the web endpoints should still work.

Define Data Models

First, define the data that we'll be passing among levels. Our *domain* contains explorers and creatures, so let's define minimal initial Pydantic models for them. Other ideas might come up later, like expeditions, journals, or ecommerce sales of coffee mugs. But for now, just include the two breathing (usually, in the case of creatures) models in Example 8-10.

Example 8-10. Model definition in model/explorer.py

```
from pydantic import BaseModel

class Explorer(BaseModel):
    name: str
    country: str
    description: str
```

Example 8-11 resurrects the `Creature` definition from earlier chapters.

Example 8-11. Model definition in model/creature.py

```
from pydantic import BaseModel

class Creature(BaseModel):
    name: str
    country: str
    area: str
    description: str
    aka: str
```

These are very simple initial models. You're not using any of Pydantic's features, such as required versus optional, or constrained values. This simple code can be enhanced later without massive logic upheavals.

For country values, you'll use the ISO two-character country codes; this saves a little typing, at the cost of looking up uncommon ones.

Stub and Fake Data

Also known as *mock data*, *stubs* are canned results that are returned without calling the normal "live" modules. They're a quick way to test your routes and responses.

A *fake* is a stand-in for a real data source that performs at least some of the same functions. An example is an in-memory class that mimics a database. You'll be making some fake data in this chapter and the next few, as you fill in the code that defines the layers and their communication. In Chapter 10, you'll define an actual live data store (a database) to replace these fakes.

Create Common Functions Through the Stack

Similar to the data examples, the approach to building this site is exploratory. Often it isn't clear what will eventually be needed, so let's start with some pieces that would be common to similar sites. Providing a frontend for data usually requires ways to do the following:

- *Get* one, some, all
- *Create*
- *Replace* completely
- *Modify* partially
- *Delete*

Essentially, these are the CRUD basics from databases, although I've split the U into partial (*modify*) and complete (*replace*) functions. Maybe this distinction will prove unnecessary! It depends on where the data leads.

Create Fake Data

Working top-down, you'll duplicate some functions in all three levels. To save typing, Example 8-12 introduces the top-level directory called *fake*, with modules providing fake data on explorers and creatures.

Example 8-12. New module fake/explorer.py

```
from model.explorer import Explorer

# fake data, replaced in Chapter 10 by a real database and SQL
_explorers = [
```

```
    Explorer(name="Claude Hande",
             country="FR",
             description="Scarce during full moons"),
    Explorer(name="Noah Weiser",
             country="DE",
             description="Myopic machete man"),
    ]

def get_all() -> list[Explorer]:
    """Return all explorers"""
    return _explorers

def get_one(name: str) -> Explorer | None:
    for _explorer in _explorers:
        if _explorer.name == name:
            return _explorer
    return None

# The following are nonfunctional for now,
# so they just act like they work, without modifying
# the actual fake _explorers list:
def create(explorer: Explorer) -> Explorer:
    """Add an explorer"""
    return explorer

def modify(explorer: Explorer) -> Explorer:
    """Partially modify an explorer"""
    return explorer

def replace(explorer: Explorer) -> Explorer:
    """Completely replace an explorer"""
    return explorer

def delete(name: str) -> bool:
    """Delete an explorer; return None if it existed"""
    return None
```

The creature setup in Example 8-13 is similar.

Example 8-13. New module fake/creature.py

```
from model.creature import Creature


# fake data, until we use a real database and SQL
_creatures = [
    Creature(name="Yeti",
             aka="Abominable Snowman",
             country="CN",
             area="Himalayas",
             description="Hirsute Himalayan"),
```

```
    Creature(name="Bigfoot",
            description="Yeti's Cousin Eddie",
            country="US",
            area="*",
            aka="Sasquatch"),
    ]

def get_all() -> list[Creature]:
    """Return all creatures"""
    return _creatures

def get_one(name: str) -> Creature | None:
    """Return one creature"""
    for _creature in _creatures:
        if _creature.name == name:
            return _creature
    return None

# The following are nonfunctional for now,
# so they just act like they work, without modifying
# the actual fake _creatures list:
def create(creature: Creature) -> Creature:
    """Add a creature"""
    return creature

def modify(creature: Creature) -> Creature:
    """Partially modify a creature"""
    return creature

def replace(creature: Creature) -> Creature:
    """Completely replace a creature"""
    return creature

def delete(name: str):
    """Delete a creature; return None if it existed"""
    return None
```

 Yes, the module functions are almost identical. They'll change later, when a real database arrives and must handle the differing fields of the two models. Also, you're using separate functions here, rather than defining a Fake class or abstract class. A module has its own namespace, so it's an equivalent way of bundling data and functions.

Now let's modify the web functions from Examples 8-12 and 8-13. Preparing to build out the later layers (Service and Data), import the fake data provider that was just defined, but name it service here: import fake.explorer as service (Example 8-14). In Chapter 9, you'll do the following:

- Make a new *service/explorer.py* file.

- Import the fake data there.

- Make *web/explorer.py* import the new service module instead of the fake module.

In Chapter 10, you'll do the same in the Data layer. All of this is just adding parts and wiring them together, with as little code rework as possible. You don't turn on the electricity (i.e., a live database and persistent data) until later in Chapter 10.

Example 8-14. New endpoints for web/explorer.py

```python
from fastapi import APIRouter
from model.explorer import Explorer
import fake.explorer as service

router = APIRouter(prefix = "/explorer")

@router.get("/")
def get_all() -> list[Explorer]:
    return service.get_all()

@router.get("/{name}")
def get_one(name) -> Explorer | None:
    return service.get_one(name)

# all the remaining endpoints do nothing yet:
@router.post("/")
def create(explorer: Explorer) -> Explorer:
    return service.create(explorer)

@router.patch("/")
def modify(explorer: Explorer) -> Explorer:
    return service.modify(explorer)

@router.put("/")
def replace(explorer: Explorer) -> Explorer:
    return service.replace(explorer)

@router.delete("/{name}")
def delete(name: str):
    return None
```

And now, do the same for */creature* endpoints (Example 8-15). Yes, this is similar cut-and-paste code for now, but doing this up front simplifies changes later on—and there will always be changes later.

Example 8-15. New endpoints for web/creature.py

```python
from fastapi import APIRouter
from model.creature import Creature
import fake.creature as service

router = APIRouter(prefix = "/creature")

@router.get("/")
def get_all() -> list[Creature]:
    return service.get_all()

@router.get("/{name}")
def get_one(name) -> Creature:
    return service.get_one(name)

# all the remaining endpoints do nothing yet:
@router.post("/")
def create(creature: Creature) -> Creature:
    return service.create(creature)

@router.patch("/")
def modify(creature: Creature) -> Creature:
    return service.modify(creature)

@router.put("/")
def replace(creature: Creature) -> Creature:
    return service.replace(creature)

@router.delete("/{name}")
def delete(name: str):
    return service.delete(name)
```

The last time we poked at *main.py*, it was to add the subrouter for */explorer* URLs. Now, let's add another for */creature* in Example 8-16.

Example 8-16. Add creature subrouter to main.py

```python
import uvicorn
from fastapi import FastAPI
from web import explorer, creature

app = FastAPI()

app.include_router(explorer.router)
app.include_router(creature.router)

if __name__ == "__main__":
    uvicorn.run("main:app", reload=True)
```

Did all of that work? If you typed or pasted everything exactly, Uvicorn should have restarted the application. Let's try some manual tests.

Test!

Chapter 12 will show how to use pytest to automate testing at various levels. Examples 8-17 to 8-21 perform some manual Web-layer tests of the explorer endpoints with HTTPie.

Example 8-17. Test the Get All endpoint

```
$ http -b localhost:8000/explorer/
[
    {
        "country": "FR",
        "name": "Claude Hande",
        "description": "Scarce during full moons"
    },
    {
        "country": "DE",
        "name": "Noah Weiser",
        "description": "Myopic machete man"
    }
]
```

Example 8-18. Test the Get One endpoint

```
$ http -b localhost:8000/explorer/"Noah Weiser"
{
    "country": "DE",
    "name": "Noah Weiser",
    "description": "Myopic machete man"
}
```

Example 8-19. Test the Replace endpoint

```
$ http -b PUT localhost:8000/explorer/"Noah Weiser"
{
    "country": "DE",
    "name": "Noah Weiser",
    "description": "Myopic machete man"
}
```

Example 8-20. Test the Modify endpoint

```
$ http -b PATCH localhost:8000/explorer/"Noah Weiser"
{
    "country": "DE",
```

```
    "name": "Noah Weiser",
    "description": "Myopic machete man"
}
```

Example 8-21. Test the Delete endpoint

```
$ http -b DELETE localhost:8000/explorer/Noah%20Weiser
true

$ http -b DELETE localhost:8000/explorer/Edmund%20Hillary
false
```

You can do the same for the */creature* endpoints.

Using the FastAPI Automated Test Forms

Besides the manual tests that I've used in most examples, FastAPI provides very nice automated test forms at the endpoints */docs* and */redocs*. They're two different styles for the same information, so I'll just show a little from the */docs* pages in Figure 8-1.

Figure 8-1. Generated documentation page

Try the first test:

1. Click the down-arrow to the right under the top GET /explorer/ section. That will open up a large light blue form.

2. Click the blue Execute button on the left. You'll see the top section of the results in Figure 8-2.

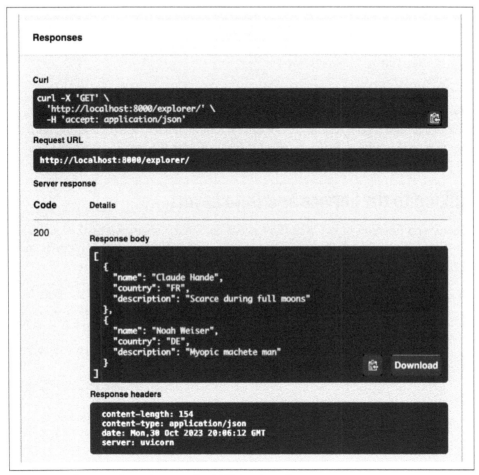

Figure 8-2. Generated results page for GET /explorer/

In the lower "Response body" section, you'll see the JSON returned for the (fake) explorer data that you've defined so far:

```
[
  {
    "name": "Claude Hande",
    "country": "FE",
    "description": "Scarce during full moons"
  },
  {
    "name": "Noah Weiser",
    "country": "DE",
    "description": "Myopic machete man"
  }
]
```

Try all the others. For some (like `GET /explorer/{name}`), you'll need to provide an input value. You'll get a response for each, even though a few still do nothing until the database code is added. You can repeat these tests near the end of Chapters 9 and 10 to ensure that no data pipelines were punctured during these code changes.

Talking to the Service and Data Layers

Whenever a function in the Web layer needs data that is managed by the Data layer, that function should ask the Service layer to be an intermediary. This requires more code and may seem unnecessary, but it's a good idea:

- As the label on the jar says, the Web layer deals with the web, and the Data layer deals with external data stores and services. It's much safer to keep their respective details completely separate.

- The layers can be tested independently. Separation of layer mechanisms allows this.

 For a very small site, you could skip the Service layer if it doesn't add any value. Chapter 9 initially defines service functions that do little more than pass requests and responses between the Web and Data layers. At least keep the Web and Data layers separate, though.

What does that Service layer function do? You'll see in the next chapter. Hint: it talks to the Data layer, but in a hushed voice so the Web layer doesn't know exactly what it's saying. But it also defines any specific business logic, such as interactions between resources. Mainly, the Web and Data layers should not care what's going on in there. (The Service layer is a Secret Service.)

Pagination and Sorting

In web interfaces, when returning many or all things with URL patterns like GET */resource*, you often want to request the lookup and return of the following:

- Only one thing
- Possibly many things
- All things

How do you get our well-meaning but extremely literal-minded computer to do these things? Well, for the first case, the RESTful pattern that I mentioned earlier is to include the resource's ID in the URL path. When getting multiple resources, we may want to see the results in a particular order:

Sort
> Order all the results, even if you get only a set of them at a time.

Paginate
> Return only some results at a time, respecting any sorting.

In each case, a group of user-specified parameters indicates what you want. It's common to provide these as query parameters. Here are some examples:

Sort
> GET /explorer?sort=country: Get all explorers, sorted by country code.

Paginate
> GET /explorer?offset=10&size=10: Return (in this case, unsorted) explorers in places 10 through 19 of the whole list.

Both
> GET /explorer?sort=country&offset=10&size=10

Although you could specify these as individual query parameters, FastAPI's dependency injection can help:

- Define the sort and paginate parameters as a Pydantic model.
- Provide the parameters model to the get_all() path function with the Depends feature in the path function arguments.

Where should the sorting and pagination occur? At first, it may seem simplest for the database queries to pass full results up to the Web layer, and use Python to carve up the data there. But that isn't very efficient. These tasks usually fit best in the Data layer, because databases are good at those things. I'll finally get around to some code for these in Chapter 17, which has more database tidbits beyond those in Chapter 10.

Review

This chapter filled out more details from Chapter 3 and others. It began the process of making a full site for information on imaginary creatures and their explorers. Starting with the Web layer, you defined endpoints with FastAPI path decorators and path functions. The path functions gather request data from wherever they live in the HTTP request bytes. Model data is automatically checked and validated by Pydantic. Path functions generally pass arguments to corresponding service functions, which are coming in the next chapter.

## CHAPTER 9

Service Layer

What was that middle thing?
—Otto West, *A Fish Called Wanda*

Preview

This chapter expands on the Service layer—the middle thing. A leaky roof can cost a lot of money. Leaky software isn't as obvious but can cost a lot of time and effort. How can you structure your application so that the layers don't leak? In particular, what should and should not go into the Service layer in the middle?

Defining a Service

The Service layer is the heart of the website, its reason for being. It takes requests from multiple sources, accesses the data that is the DNA of the site, and returns responses.

Common service patterns include a combination of the following:

- Create / retrieve / change (partially or completely) / delete
- One thing / multiple things

At the RESTful router layer, the nouns are *resources*. In this book, our resources will initially include cryptids (imaginary creatures) and people (cryptid explorers).

Later, it will be possible to define related resources like these:

- Places
- Events (e.g., expeditions, sightings)

Layout

Here's the current file and directory layout:

```
main.py
web
├── __init__.py
├── creature.py
├── explorer.py
service
├── __init__.py
├── creature.py
├── explorer.py
data
├── __init__.py
├── creature.py
├── explorer.py
model
├── __init__.py
├── creature.py
├── explorer.py
fake
├── __init__.py
├── creature.py
├── explorer.py
└── test
```

In this chapter, you'll fiddle with files in the *service* directory.

Protection

One nice thing about layers is that you don't have to worry about everything. The Service layer cares only about what goes into and out of the data. As you'll see in Chapter 11, a higher layer (in this book, *Web*) can handle the authentication and authorization messiness. The functions to create, modify, and delete should not be wide open, and even the get functions might eventually need some limits.

Functions

Let's start with *creature.py*. At this point, the needs of *explorer.py* will be almost the same, and we can borrow almost everything. It's so tempting to write a single service file that handles both, but, almost inevitably, at some point we'll need to handle them differently.

Also at this point, the service file is pretty much a pass-through layer. This is a case in which a little extra structure at the start will pay off later. Much as you did for *web/creature.py* and *web/explorer.py* in Chapter 8, you'll define service modules for both, and hook both of them up to their corresponding *fake* data modules for now (Examples 9-1 and 9-2).

Example 9-1. An initial service/creature.py *file*

```
from models.creature import Creature
import fake.creature as data

def get_all() -> list[Creature]:
    return data.get_all()

def get_one(name: str) -> Creature | None:
    return data.get(id)

def create(creature: Creature) -> Creature:
    return data.create(creature)

def replace(id, creature: Creature) -> Creature:
    return data.replace(id, creature)

def modify(id, creature: Creature) -> Creature:
    return data.modify(id, creature)

def delete(id, creature: Creature) -> bool:
    return data.delete(id)
```

Example 9-2. An initial service/explorer.py *file*

```
from models.explorer import Explorer
import fake.explorer as data

def get_all() -> list[Explorer]:
    return data.get_all()

def get_one(name: str) -> Explorer | None:
    return data.get(name)

def create(explorer: Explorer) -> Explorer:
    return data.create(explorer)

def replace(id, explorer: Explorer) -> Explorer:
    return data.replace(id, explorer)

def modify(id, explorer: Explorer) -> Explorer:
    return data.modify(id, explorer)

def delete(id, explorer: Explorer) -> bool:
    return data.delete(id)
```

The syntax of the `get_one()` function's return value (`Creature | None`) needs at least Python 3.9. For earlier versions, you need `Optional`:

```
from typing import Optional
...
def get_one(name: str) -> Optional[Creature]:
...
```

Test!

Now that the codebase is filling out a bit, it's a good time to introduce automated tests. (The Web tests in the previous chapter have all been manual tests.) So let's make some directories:

test
> A top-level directory, alongside *web*, *service*, *data*, and *model*.

> *unit*
>> Exercise single functions, but don't cross layer boundaries.

>> *web*
>>> Web-layer unit tests.

>> *service*
>>> Service-layer unit tests.

>> *data*
>>> Data-layer unit tests.

> *full*
>> Also known as *end-to-end* or *contract* tests, these span all layers at once. They address the API endpoints in the Web layer.

The directories have the *test_* prefix or *_test* suffix for use by pytest, which you'll start to see in Example 9-4 (which runs the test in Example 9-3).

Before testing, a few API design choices need to be made. What should be returned by the `get_one()` function if a matching `Creature` or `Explorer` isn't found? You can return `None`, as in Example 9-2. Or you could raise an exception. None of the built-in Python exception types deal directly with missing values:

- `TypeError` may be the closest, because `None` is a different type than `Creature`.
- `ValueError` is more suited for the wrong value for a given type, but I guess you could say that passing a missing string `id` to `get_one(id)` qualifies.
- You could define your own `MissingError` if you really want to.

Whichever method you choose, the effects will bubble up all the way to the top layer.

Let's go with the None alternative rather than the exception for now. After all, that's what *none* means. Example 9-3 is a test.

Example 9-3. Service test test/unit/service/test_creature.py

```
from model.creature import Creature
from service import creature as code

sample = Creature(name="yeti",
        country="CN",
        area="Himalayas",
        description="Hirsute Himalayan",
        aka="Abominable Snowman",
        )

def test_create():
    resp = code.create(sample)
    assert resp == sample

def test_get_exists():
    resp = code.get_one("yeti")
    assert resp == sample

def test_get_missing():
    resp = code.get_one("boxturtle")
    assert data is None
```

Run the test in Example 9-4.

Example 9-4. Run the service test

```
$ pytest -v test/unit/service/test_creature.py
test_creature.py::test_create PASSED                    [ 16%]
test_creature.py::test_get_exists PASSED                [ 50%]
test_creature.py::test_get_missing PASSED               [ 66%]

========================= 3 passed in 0.06s =========================
```

In Chapter 10, get_one() will no longer return None for a missing creature, and the test_get_missing() test in Example 9-4 would fail. But that will be fixed.

Other Service-Level Stuff

We're in the middle of the stack now—the part that really defines our site's purpose. And so far, we've used it only to forward web requests to the (next chapter's) Data layer.

So far, this book has developed the site iteratively, building a minimal base for future work. As you learn more about what you have, what you can do, and what users might want, you can branch out and experiment. Some ideas might benefit only larger sites, but here are some technical site-helper ideas:

- Logging
- Metrics
- Monitoring
- Tracing

This section discusses each of these. We'll revisit these options in "Troubleshooting" on page 190, to see if they can help diagnose problems.

Logging

FastAPI logs each API call to an endpoint—including the timestamp, method, and URL—but not any data delivered via the body or headers.

Metrics, Monitoring, Observability

If you run a website, you probably want to know how it's doing. For an API website, you might want to know which endpoints are being accessed, how many people are visiting, and so on. Statistics on such factors are called *metrics*, and the gathering of them is *monitoring* or *observability*.

Popular metrics tools nowadays include Prometheus (*https://prometheus.io*) for gathering metrics and Grafana (*https://grafana.com*) for displaying metrics.

Tracing

How well is your site performing? It's common for metrics to be good overall, but with disappointing results here or there. Or the whole site may be a mess. Either way, it's useful to have a tool that measures how long an API call takes, end to end—and not just overall time, but the time for each intermediate step. If something's slow, you can find the weak link in the chain. This is *tracing*.

A new open source project has taken earlier tracing products like Jaeger (*https:// www.jaegertracing.io*) and branded them as OpenTelemetry (*https://opentelemetry.io*).

It has a Python API (*https://oreil.ly/gyL70*) and at least one integration with FastAPI (*https://oreil.ly/L6RXV*).

To install and configure OpenTelemetry with Python, follow the instructions in the OpenTelemetry Python documentation (*https://oreil.ly/MBgd5*).

Other

These production issues will be discussed in Chapter 13. Besides these, what about our domain—cryptids and anything associated with them? Besides bare details on explorers and creatures, what else might you want to take on? You may come up with new ideas that require changes to the models and other layers. Here are some ideas you might try:

- Links of explorers to the creatures that they seek
- Sighting data
- Expeditions
- Photos and videos
- Sasquatch mugs and T-shirts (Figure 9-1)

Figure 9-1. A word from our sponsor

Each of these categories will generally require one or more new models to be defined, and new modules and functions. Some will be added in Part IV, which is a gallery of applications added to the base built here in Part III.

Review

In this chapter, you replicated some functions from the Web layer and moved the fake data that they worked with. The goal was to initiate the new Service layer. So far, it's been a cookie-cutter process, but it will evolve and diverge after this. The next chapter builds the final Data layer, yielding a truly live website.

## CHAPTER 10

Data Layer

If I'm not mistaken, I think Data was the comic relief on the show.

—Brent Spiner, *Star Trek: The Next Generation*

Preview

This chapter finally creates a persistent home for our site's data, at last connecting the three layers. It uses the relational database SQLite and introduces Python's database API, aptly named DB-API. Chapter 14 goes into much more detail on databases, including the SQLAlchemy package and nonrelational databases.

DB-API

For over 20 years, Python has included a basic definition for a relational database interface called DB-API: PEP 249 (*https://oreil.ly/4Gp9T*). Anyone who writes a Python driver for a relational database is expected to at least include support for DB-API, although other features may be included.

These are the main DB-API functions:

- Create a connection conn to the database with connect().
- Create a cursor curs with conn.cursor().
- Execute a SQL string stmt with curs.execute(stmt).

The execute...() functions run a SQL statement *stmt* string with optional parameters, listed here:

- execute(*stmt*) if there are no parameters
- execute(*stmt*, *params*), with parameters *params* in a single sequence (list or tuple) or dict
- executemany(*stmt*, *params_seq*), with multiple parameter groups in the sequence *params_seq*

There are five ways of specifying parameters, and not all are supported by all database drivers. If we have a statement *stmt* that begins with "select * from creature where", and we want to specify string parameters for the creature's name *or* country, the rest of the *stmt* string and its parameters would look like those in Table 10-1.

Table 10-1. Specifying the statement and parameters

Type	Statement part	Parameters part
qmark	name=? or country=?	(*name*, *country*)
numeric	name=:0 or country=:1	(*name*, *country*)
format	name=%s or country=%s	(*name*, *country*)
named	name=:name or country=:country	{"name": *name*, "country": *country*}
pyformat	name=%(name)s or country=%(country)s	{"name": *name*, "country": *country*}

The first three take a tuple argument, where the parameter order matches the ?, :N, or %s in the statement. The last two take a dictionary, where the keys match the names in the statement.

So, the full call for the *named* style would look like Example 10-1.

Example 10-1. Using named-style parameters.

```
stmt = """select * from creature where
    name=:name or country=:country"""
params = {"name": "yeti", "country": "CN"}
curs.execute(stmt, params)
```

For SQL INSERT, DELETE, and UPDATE statements, the returned value from execute() tells you how it worked. For SELECT, you iterate over returned data row(s), as Python tuples, with a fetch method:

- fetchone() returns one tuple, or None.
- fetchall() returns a sequence of tuples.
- fetchmany(*num*) returns up to *num* tuples.

SQLite

Python includes support for one database (SQLite (*https://www.sqlite.org*)) with the module sqlite3 (*https://oreil.ly/CcYtJ*) in its standard packages.

SQLite is unusual: it has no separate database server. All the code is in a library, and storage is in a single file. Other databases run separate servers, and clients communicate with them over TCP/IP, using specific protocols. Let's use SQLite as the first physical data store for this website. Chapter 14 will include other databases, relational and not, as well as more advanced packages like SQLAlchemy and techniques like ORMs.

First, we need to define how the data structures we've been using in the website (*models*) can be represented in the database. So far, our only models have been simple and similar, but not identical: Creature and Explorer. They will change as we think of more things to do with them and let the data evolve without massive code changes.

Example 10-2 shows the bare DB-API code and SQL to create and work with the first tables. It uses *named* argument strings (values are represented like *name*), which are supported by the sqlite3 package.

Example 10-2. Create the file data/creature.py *using sqlite3*

```
import sqlite3
from model.creature import Creature

DB_NAME = "cryptid.db"
conn = sqlite3.connect(DB_NAME)
curs = conn.cursor()

def init():
    curs.execute("create table creature(name, description, country, area, aka)")

def row_to_model(row: tuple) -> Creature:
    name, description, country, area, aka = row
    return Creature(name, description, country, area, aka)

def model_to_dict(creature: Creature) -> dict:
```

```
        return creature.dict()

def get_one(name: str) -> Creature:
    qry = "select * from creature where name=:name"
    params = {"name": name}
    curs.execute(qry, params)
    row = curs.fetchone()
    return row_to_model(row)

def get_all(name: str) -> list[Creature]:
    qry = "select * from creature"
    curs.execute(qry)
    rows = list(curs.fetchall())
    return [row_to_model(row) for row in rows]

def create(creature: Creature):
    qry = """insert into creature values
        (:name, :description, :country, :area, :aka)"""
    params = model_to_dict(creature)
    curs.execute(qry, params)

def modify(creature: Creature):
    return creature

def replace(creature: Creature):
    return creature

def delete(creature: Creature):
    qry = "delete from creature where name = :name"
    params = {"name": creature.name}
    curs.execute(qry, params)
```

Near the top, the init() function makes the connection to sqlite3 and the database fake *cryptid.db*. It stores this in the variable conn; this is global within the *data/creature.py* module. Next, the curs variable is a *cursor* for iterating over data returned by executing a SQL SELECT statement; it's also global to the module.

Two utility functions translate between Pydantic models and DB-API:

- row_to_model() converts a tuple returned by a *fetch* function to a model object.
- model_to_dict() translates a Pydantic model to a dictionary, suitable for use as a *named* query parameter.

The fake CRUD functions that have been present so far in each layer down (Web → Service → Data) will now be replaced. They use only plain SQL and the DB-API methods in sqlite3.

Layout

So far, (fake) data has been modified in steps:

1. In Chapter 8, we made the fake *creatures* list in *web/creature.py*.
2. In Chapter 8, we made the fake *explorers* list in *web/explorer.py*.
3. In Chapter 9, we moved fake *creatures* to *service/creature.py*.
4. In Chapter 9, we moved fake *explorers* to *service/explorer.py*.

Now the data has moved for the last time, down to *data/creature.py*. But it's not fake anymore: it's real live data, persisting in the SQLite database file *cryptids.db*. Creature data, again by lack of imagination, is stored in the SQL table `creature` in this database.

Once you save this new file, Uvicorn should restart from your top *main.py*, which calls *web/creature.py*, which calls *service/creature.py*, and finally down to this new *data/creature.py*.

Making It Work

We have one small problem: this module never calls its `init()` function, so there's no SQLite `conn` or `curs` for the other functions to use. This a configuration issue: how do we provide the database information at startup time? Possibilities include the following:

- Hardwiring the database info in the code, as in Example 10-2.
- Passing the info down through the layers. But this would violate the separation of layers; the Web and Service layers should not know the internals of the Data layer.
- Passing the info from a different external source, such as
  - A config file
  - An environment variable

The environment variable is simple and is endorsed by recommendations like the Twelve-Factor App (*https://12factor.net/config*). The code can include a default value if the environment variable isn't specified. This approach can also be used in testing, to provide a separate test database from the production one.

In Example 10-3, let's define an environment variable called `CRYPTID_SQLITE_DB`, with the default value `cryptid.db`. Make a new file called *data/init.py* for the new database initialization code so it can also be reused for the explorer code.

Example 10-3. New data initialization module data/init.py

```python
"""Initialize SQLite database"""

import os
from pathlib import Path
from sqlite3 import connect, Connection, Cursor, IntegrityError

conn: Connection | None = None
curs: Cursor | None = None

def get_db(name: str|None = None, reset: bool = False):
    """Connect to SQLite database file"""
    global conn, curs
    if conn:
        if not reset:
            return
        conn = None
    if not name:
        name = os.getenv("CRYPTID_SQLITE_DB")
        top_dir = Path(__file__).resolve().parents[1] # repo top
        db_dir = top_dir / "db"
        db_name = "cryptid.db"
        db_path = str(db_dir / db_name)
        name = os.getenv("CRYPTID_SQLITE_DB", db_path)
    conn = connect(name, check_same_thread=False)
    curs = conn.cursor()

get_db()
```

A Python module is a *singleton*, called only once despite multiple imports. So, the initialization code in *init.py* is run only once, when the first import of it occurs.

Last, modify *data/creature.py* in Example 10-4 to use this new module instead:

- Mainly, drop lines 4 through 8.

- Oh, and create the `creature` table in the first place!

- The table fields are all SQL `text` strings. This is the default column type in SQLite (unlike most SQL databases), so you didn't need to include `text` earlier, but being explicit doesn't hurt.

- The `if not exists` avoids clobbering the table after it's been created.

- The `name` field is the explicit `primary key` for this table. If this table ever houses lots of explorer data, that key will be necessary for fast lookups. The alternative is the dreaded *table scan*, where the database code needs to look at every row until it finds a match for `name`.

Example 10-4. Add database configuration to data/creature.py

```python
from .init import conn, curs
from model.creature import Creature

curs.execute("""create table if not exists creature(
                name text primary key,
                description text,
                country text,
                area text,
                aka text)""")

def row_to_model(row: tuple) -> Creature:
    (name, description, country, area, aka) = row
    return Creature(name, description, country, area, aka)

def model_to_dict(creature: Creature) -> dict:
    return creature.dict()

def get_one(name: str) -> Creature:
    qry = "select * from creature where name=:name"
    params = {"name": name}
    curs.execute(qry, params)
    return row_to_model(curs.fetchone())

def get_all() -> list[Creature]:
    qry = "select * from creature"
    curs.execute(qry)
    return [row_to_model(row) for row in curs.fetchall()]

def create(creature: Creature) -> Creature:
    qry = "insert into creature values"
          "(:name, :description, :country, :area, :aka)"
    params = model_to_dict(creature)
    curs.execute(qry, params)
    return get_one(creature.name)

def modify(creature: Creature) -> Creature:
    qry = """update creature
            set country=:country,
                name=:name,
                description=:description,
                area=:area,
                aka=:aka
            where name=:name_orig"""
    params = model_to_dict(creature)
    params["name_orig"] = creature.name
    _ = curs.execute(qry, params)
    return get_one(creature.name)

def delete(creature: Creature) -> bool:
    qry = "delete from creature where name = :name"
```

```
    params = {"name": creature.name}
    res = curs.execute(qry, params)
    return bool(res)
```

By importing conn and curs from *init.py*, it's no longer necessary for *data/creature.py* to import sqlite3 itself—unless someday it's necessary to call another sqlite3 method that isn't a method of the conn or curs objects.

Again, these changes should goose Uvicorn into reloading everything. From now on, testing with any of the methods that you've seen so far (HTTPie and friends, or the automated /docs forms) will show data that persists. If you add a creature, it will be there the next time you get all of them.

Let's do the same for explorers in Example 10-5.

Example 10-5. Add database configuration to data/explorer.py

```
from .init import curs
from model.explorer import Explorer


curs.execute("""create table if not exists explorer(
                name text primary key,
                country text,
                description text)""")

def row_to_model(row: tuple) -> Explorer:
    return Explorer(name=row[0], country=row[1], description=row[2])

def model_to_dict(explorer: Explorer) -> dict:
    return explorer.dict() if explorer else None

def get_one(name: str) -> Explorer:
    qry = "select * from explorer where name=:name"
    params = {"name": name}
    curs.execute(qry, params)
    return row_to_model(curs.fetchone())

def get_all() -> list[Explorer]:
    qry = "select * from explorer"
    curs.execute(qry)
    return [row_to_model(row) for row in curs.fetchall()]

def create(explorer: Explorer) -> Explorer:
    qry = """insert into explorer (name, country, description)
            values (:name, :country, :description)"""
    params = model_to_dict(explorer)
    _ = curs.execute(qry, params)
    return get_one(explorer.name)

def modify(name: str, explorer: Explorer) -> Explorer:
```

```
    qry = """update explorer
            set country=:country,
            name=:name,
            description=:description
            where name=:name_orig"""
    params = model_to_dict(explorer)
    params["name_orig"] = explorer.name
    _ = curs.execute(qry, params)
    explorer2 = get_one(explorer.name)
    return explorer2

def delete(explorer: Explorer) -> bool:
    qry = "delete from explorer where name = :name"
    params = {"name": explorer.name}
    res = curs.execute(qry, params)
    return bool(res)
```

Test!

That's a lot of code with no tests. Does everything work? I'd be surprised if it all did. So let's set up some tests.

Make these subdirectories under the *test* directory:

unit
    Within a layer

full
    Across all layers

Which type should you write and run first? Most people write automated unit tests first; they're smaller, and all the other layer pieces may not exist yet. In this book, development has been top-down, and we're now completing the last layer. Also, we did manual tests (with HTTPie and friends) in Chapters 8 and 9. Those helped to expose bugs and omissions quickly; automated tests ensure that you don't keep making the same errors later. So, I recommend the following:

- Some manual tests as you're first writing the code
- Unit tests after you've fixed Python syntax errors
- Full tests after you have a full data flow across all layers

Full Tests

These call the web endpoints, which take the code elevator down through Service to Data, and back up again. Sometimes these are called *end-to-end* or *contract* tests.

Get all explorers

Dipping a toe in the test waters, not yet knowing if they're infested with piranhas, is brave volunteer Example 10-6.

Example 10-6. The Get All Explorers test

```
$ http localhost:8000/explorer
HTTP/1.1 405 Method Not Allowed
allow: POST
content-length: 31
content-type: application/json
date: Mon, 27 Feb 2023 20:05:18 GMT
server: uvicorn

{
    "detail": "Method Not Allowed"
}
```

Eek! What happened?

Oh. The test asked for /explorer, not /explorer/, and there's no GET-method path function for the URL *explorer* (with no final slash). In *web/explorer.py*, the path decorator for the get_all() path function is this:

```
@router.get("/")
```

That, plus the earlier code

```
router = APIRouter(prefix = "/explorer")
```

means this get_all() path function serves a URL containing */explorer/*.

Example 10-7 happily shows that you can have more than one path decorator per path function.

Example 10-7. Add a nonslash path decorator for the get_all() path function

```
@router.get("")
@router.get("/")
def get_all() -> list[Explorer]:
    return service.get_all()
```

Test with both URLs in Examples 10-8 and 10-9.

Example 10-8. Test the nonslash endpoint

```
$ http localhost:8000/explorer
HTTP/1.1 200 OK
content-length: 2
```

```
content-type: application/json
date: Mon, 27 Feb 2023 20:12:44 GMT
server: uvicorn
```

[]

Example 10-9. Test the slash endpoint

```
$ http localhost:8000/explorer/
HTTP/1.1 200 OK
content-length: 2
content-type: application/json
date: Mon, 27 Feb 2023 20:14:39 GMT
server: uvicorn
```

[]

Now that both of these work, create an explorer, and retry the Get All test after. Example 10-10 attempts this, but with a plot twist.

Example 10-10. Test explorer creation, with an input error

```
$ http post localhost:8000/explorer name="Beau Buffette", contry="US"
HTTP/1.1 422 Unprocessable Entity
content-length: 95
content-type: application/json
date: Mon, 27 Feb 2023 20:17:45 GMT
server: uvicorn

{
    "detail": [
        {
            "loc": [
                "body",
                "country"
            ],
            "msg": "field required",
            "type": "value_error.missing"
        }
    ]
}
```

I misspelled country, although my speling is usually impeckable. Pydantic caught this in the Web layer, returning a 422 HTTP status code and a description of the problem. Generally, if FastAPI returns a 422, the odds are that Pydantic fingered the perpetrator. The "loc" part says where the error occurred: the field "country" is missing, because I'm such an inept typist.

Fix the spelling and retest in Example 10-11.

Example 10-11. Create an explorer with the corrected value

```
$ http post localhost:8000/explorer name="Beau Buffette" country="US"
HTTP/1.1 201 Created
content-length: 55
content-type: application/json
date: Mon, 27 Feb 2023 20:20:49 GMT
server: uvicorn

{
    "name": "Beau Buffette,",
    "country": "US",
    "description": ""
}
```

This time the call returns a 201 status code, which is traditional when a resource is created (all 2*xx* status codes are considered to indicate success, with plain 200 being the most generic). The response also contains the JSON version of the Explorer object that was just created.

Now back to the initial test: will Beau turn up in the Get All Explorers test? Example 10-12 answers this burning question.

Example 10-12. Did the latest create() work?

```
$ http localhost:8000/explorer
HTTP/1.1 200 OK
content-length: 57
content-type: application/json
date: Mon, 27 Feb 2023 20:26:26 GMT
server: uvicorn

[
    {
        "name": "Beau Buffette",
        "country": "US",
        "description": ""
    }
]
```

Yay.

Get one explorer

Now, what happens if you try to look up Beau with the Get One endpoint (Example 10-13)?

Example 10-13. Test the Get One endpoint

```
$ http localhost:8000/explorer/"Beau Buffette"
HTTP/1.1 200 OK
content-length: 55
content-type: application/json
date: Mon, 27 Feb 2023 20:28:48 GMT
server: uvicorn

{
    "name": "Beau Buffette",
    "country": "US",
    "description": ""
}
```

I used the quotes to preserve that space between the first and last names. In URLs, you could also use `Beau%20Buffette`; the `%20` is the hex code for the space character in ASCII.

Missing and duplicate data

I've ignored two main error classes so far:

Missing data
> If you try to get, modify, or delete an explorer by a name that isn't in the database.

Duplicate data
> If you try to create an explorer with the same name more than once.

So, what if you ask for a nonexistent or duplicate explorer? So far, the code has been too optimistic, and exceptions will bubble up from the abyss.

Our friend Beau was just added to the database. Imagine his evil clone (who shares his name) plots to replace him some dark night, using Example 10-14.

Example 10-14. Duplicate error: try to create an explorer more than once

```
$ http post localhost:8000/explorer name="Beau Buffette" country="US"
HTTP/1.1 500 Internal Server Error
content-length: 3127
content-type: text/plain; charset=utf-8
date: Mon, 27 Feb 2023 21:04:09 GMT
server: uvicorn

Traceback (most recent call last):
  File ".../starlette/middleware/errors.py", line 162, in call
... (lots of confusing innards here) ...
  File ".../service/explorer.py", line 11, in create
    return data.create(explorer)
           ^^^^^^^
```

```
      File ".../data/explorer.py", line 37, in create
        curs.execute(qry, params)
    sqlite3.IntegrityError: UNIQUE constraint failed: explorer.name
```

I omitted most of the lines in that error trace (and replaced some parts with ellipses), because it contained mostly internal calls made by FastAPI and the underlying Starlette. But that last line: a SQLite exception in the Web layer! Where is the fainting couch?

Right on the heels of this, yet another horror in Example 10-15: a missing explorer.

Example 10-15. Get a nonexistent explorer

```
$ http localhost:8000/explorer/"Beau Buffalo"
HTTP/1.1 500 Internal Server Error
content-length: 3282
content-type: text/plain; charset=utf-8
date: Mon, 27 Feb 2023 21:09:37 GMT
server: uvicorn

Traceback (most recent call last):
  File ".../starlette/middleware/errors.py", line 162, in call
... (many lines of ancient cuneiform) ...
  File ".../data/explorer.py", line 11, in row_to_model
    name, country, description = row
    ^^^^^^^^
TypeError: cannot unpack non-iterable NoneType object
```

What's a good way to catch these at the bottom (Data) layer, and communicate the details to the top (Web)? Possibilities include the following:

- Let SQLite cough up a hairball (exception) and deal with it in the Web layer.
  - But: this mixes the layers, which is *Bad*. The Web layer should not know anything about specific databases.
- Make every function in the Service and Data layers return `Explorer | None` where they used to return `Explorer`. Then a `None` indicates failure. (You can shorten this by defining `OptExplorer = Explorer | None` in *model/explorer.py*.)
  - But: the function may have failed for more than one reason, and you might want details. And this requires lots of code editing.
- Define exceptions for `Missing` and `Duplicate` data, including details of the problem. These will flow up through the layers with no code changes until the Web path functions catch them. They're also application specific rather than database specific, preserving the sanctity of the layers.
  - But: actually, I like this one, so it goes in Example 10-16.

Example 10-16. Define a new top-level errors.py

```python
class Missing(Exception):
    def __init__(self, msg:str):
        self.msg = msg

class Duplicate(Exception):
    def __init__(self, msg:str):
        self.msg = msg
```

Each of these exceptions has a `msg` string attribute that can inform the higher-level code of what happened.

To implement this, in Example 10-17, have *data/init.py* import the DB-API exception that SQLite would raise for a duplicate.

Example 10-17. Add a SQLite exception import into data/init.py

```python
from sqlite3 import connect, IntegrityError
```

Import and catch this error in Example 10-18.

Example 10-18. Modify data/explorer.py *to catch and raise these exceptions*

```python
from init import (conn, curs, IntegrityError)
from model.explorer import Explorer
from error import Missing, Duplicate

curs.execute("""create table if not exists explorer(
                name text primary key,
                country text,
                description text)""")

def row_to_model(row: tuple) -> Explorer:
    name, country, description = row
    return Explorer(name=name,
        country=country, description=description)

def model_to_dict(explorer: Explorer) -> dict:
    return explorer.dict()

def get_one(name: str) -> Explorer:
    qry = "select * from explorer where name=:name"
    params = {"name": name}
    curs.execute(qry, params)
    row = curs.fetchone()
    if row:
        return row_to_model(row)
    else:
        raise Missing(msg=f"Explorer {name} not found")
```

```
def get_all() -> list[Explorer]:
    qry = "select * from explorer"
    curs.execute(qry)
    return [row_to_model(row) for row in curs.fetchall()]

def create(explorer: Explorer) -> Explorer:
    if not explorer: return None
    qry = """insert into explorer (name, country, description) values
            (:name, :country, :description)"""
    params = model_to_dict(explorer)
    try:
        curs.execute(qry, params)
    except IntegrityError:
        raise Duplicate(msg=
            f"Explorer {explorer.name} already exists")
    return get_one(explorer.name)

def modify(name: str, explorer: Explorer) -> Explorer:
    if not (name and explorer): return None
    qry = """update explorer
            set name=:name,
            country=:country,
            description=:description
            where name=:name_orig"""
    params = model_to_dict(explorer)
    params["name_orig"] = explorer.name
    curs.execute(qry, params)
    if curs.rowcount == 1:
        return get_one(explorer.name)
    else:
        raise Missing(msg=f"Explorer {name} not found")

def delete(name: str):
    if not name: return False
    qry = "delete from explorer where name = :name"
    params = {"name": name}
    curs.execute(qry, params)
    if curs.rowcount != 1:
        raise Missing(msg=f"Explorer {name} not found")
```

This drops the need to declare that any functions return Explorer | None or
Optional[Explorer]. You indicate type hints only for normal return types, not
exceptions. Because exceptions flow upward independent of the call stack until someone catches them, for once you don't have to change anything in the Service layer. But
here's the new *web/explorer.py* in Example 10-19, with exception handlers and appropriate HTTP status code returns.

Example 10-19. Handle `Missing` *and* `Duplicate` *exceptions in* web/explorer.py

```python
from fastapi import APIRouter, HTTPException
from model.explorer import Explorer
from service import explorer as service
from error import Duplicate, Missing

router = APIRouter(prefix = "/explorer")

@router.get("")
@router.get("/")
def get_all() -> list[Explorer]:
    return service.get_all()

@router.get("/{name}")
def get_one(name) -> Explorer:
    try:
        return service.get_one(name)
    except Missing as exc:
        raise HTTPException(status_code=404, detail=exc.msg)

@router.post("", status_code=201)
@router.post("/", status_code=201)
def create(explorer: Explorer) -> Explorer:
    try:
        return service.create(explorer)
    except Duplicate as exc:
        raise HTTPException(status_code=404, detail=exc.msg)

@router.patch("/")
def modify(name: str, explorer: Explorer) -> Explorer:
    try:
        return service.modify(name, explorer)
    except Missing as exc:
        raise HTTPException(status_code=404, detail=exc.msg)

@router.delete("/{name}", status_code=204)
def delete(name: str):
    try:
        return service.delete(name)
    except Missing as exc:
        raise HTTPException(status_code=404, detail=exc.msg)
```

Test these changes in Example 10-20.

Example 10-20. Test Get One nonexisting explorer again, with new Missing exception

```
$ http localhost:8000/explorer/"Beau Buffalo"
HTTP/1.1 404 Not Found
content-length: 44
content-type: application/json
date: Mon, 27 Feb 2023 21:11:27 GMT
server: uvicorn

{
    "detail": "Explorer Beau Buffalo not found"
}
```

Good. Now, try the evil clone attempt again in Example 10-21.

Example 10-21. Test duplicate fix

```
$ http post localhost:8000/explorer name="Beau Buffette" country="US"
HTTP/1.1 404 Not Found
content-length: 50
content-type: application/json
date: Mon, 27 Feb 2023 21:14:00 GMT
server: uvicorn

{
    "detail": "Explorer Beau Buffette already exists"
}
```

The missing checks would also apply to the Modify and Delete endpoints. You can try writing similar tests for them.

Unit Tests

Unit tests deal only with the Data layer, checking the database calls and SQL syntax. I've put this section after the full tests because I wanted to have the Missing and Duplicate exceptions already defined, explained, and coded into *data/creature.py*. Example 10-22 lists the test script *test/unit/data/test_creature.py*. Here are some points to note:

- You set the environment variable CRYPTID_SQLITE_DATABASE to ":memory:" *before* importing init or creature from data. This value makes SQLite work completely in memory, not stomping any existing database file, or even creating a file on disk. It's checked in *data/init.py* when that module is first imported.

- The *fixture* named sample is passed to the functions that need a Creature object.

- The tests run in order. In this case, the same database stays up the whole time, instead of being reset between functions. The reason is to allow changes from previous functions to persist. With pytest, a fixture can have on the following:

Function scope (the default)
>   It's called anew before every test function.

Session scope
>   It's called only once, at the start.

- Some tests force the `Missing` or `Duplicate` exceptions, and verify that they caught them.

So, each of the tests in Example 10-22 gets a brand-new, unchanged `Creature` object named `sample`.

Example 10-22. Unit tests for data/creature.py

```python
import os
import pytest
from model.creature import Creature
from error import Missing, Duplicate

# set this before data imports below for data.init
os.environ["CRYPTID_SQLITE_DB"] = ":memory:"
from data import creature

@pytest.fixture
def sample() -> Creature:
    return Creature(name="yeti", country="CN", area="Himalayas",
        description="Harmless Himalayan",
        aka="Abominable Snowman")

def test_create(sample):
    resp = creature.create(sample)
    assert resp == sample

def test_create_duplicate(sample):
    with pytest.raises(Duplicate):
        _ = creature.create(sample)

def test_get_one(sample):
    resp = creature.get_one(sample.name)
    assert resp == sample

def test_get_one_missing():
    with pytest.raises(Missing):
        _ = creature.get_one("boxturtle")

def test_modify(sample):
```

```
    creature.area = "Sesame Street"
    resp = creature.modify(sample.name, sample)
    assert resp == sample

def test_modify_missing():
    thing: Creature = Creature(name="snurfle", country="RU", area="",
        description="some thing", aka="")
    with pytest.raises(Missing):
        _ = creature.modify(thing.name, thing)

def test_delete(sample):
    resp = creature.delete(sample.name)
    assert resp is None

def test_delete_missing(sample):
    with pytest.raises(Missing):
        _ = creature.delete(sample.name)
```

Hint: you can make your own version of *test/unit/data/test_explorer.py*.

Review

This chapter presented a simple data-handling layer, with a few trips up and down the layer stack as needed. Chapter 12 contains unit tests for each layer, as well as cross-layer integration and full end-to-end tests. Chapter 14 goes into more database depth and detailed examples.

## CHAPTER 11

Authentication and Authorization

Respect mah authoritay!

 —Eric Cartman, *South Park*

Preview

Sometimes a website is wide open, and any visitor can visit any page. But if any of the site's content may be modified, some endpoints will be restricted to certain people or groups. If anyone could alter pages on Amazon, imagine the odd items that would show up, and the amazing sales some people would suddenly get. Unfortunately, it's human nature—for some humans—to take advantage of the rest, who pay a hidden tax for their activities.

Should we leave our cryptid site open for any users to access any endpoint? No! Almost any sizable web service eventually needs to deal with the following:

Authentication (authn)
 Who are you?

Authorization (authz)
 What do you want?

Should the authentication and authorization (auth) code have its own new layer, say between Web and Service? Or should everything be handled by the Web or Service layer itself? This chapter dips into auth techniques and where to put them.

Often descriptions of web security seem more confusing than they need to be. Attackers can be really, really sneaky, and countermeasures may not be simple.

As I've mentioned more than once, the official FastAPI documentation is excellent. Try the Security section (*https://oreil.ly/oYsKl*) if this chapter doesn't provide as many details as you'd like.

So, let's take this walk-through in steps. I'll start with simple techniques that are intended to only hook auth into a web endpoint for testing, but would not stand up in a public website.

Interlude 1: Do You Need Authentication?

Again, *authentication* is concerned with *identity*: who are you? To implement authentication, we need a mapping of secret information to a unique identity. There are many ways to do this, with *many* variations of complexity. Let's start small and work up.

Often books and articles on web development jump right away into the details of authentication and authorization, sometimes muddling them. They sometimes skip the first question: do you really need either?

You could allow completely anonymous access to all your website's pages. But that would leave you open to exploits like denial-of-service attacks. Although some protections like rate limits can be implemented outside the web server (see Chapter 13), almost all public API providers require at least some authentication.

Beyond security, we want to know how effective websites are:

- How many unique visitors?
- What are the most popular pages?
- Do some changes increase views?
- What page sequences are common?

The answers to these questions require authentication of specific visitors. Otherwise, you can get only total counts.

If your site needs authentication or authorization, access to it should be encrypted (using HTTPS instead of HTTP), to prevent attackers from extracting secret data from plain text. See Chapter 13 for details on setting up HTTPS.

Authentication Methods

There are many web authentication methods and tools:

Username/email and password
    Using classic HTTP Basic and Digest Authentication

API key
    An opaque long string with an accompanying *secret*

OAuth2
    A set of standards for authentication and authorization

JavaScript Web Tokens (JWT)
    An encoding format containing cryptographically signed user information

In this section, I'll review the first two methods and show you how to traditionally implement them. But I'll stop before filling out the API and database code. Instead, we'll fully implement a more modern scheme with OAuth2 and JWT.

Global Authentication: Shared Secret

The very simplest authentication method is to pass a secret that's normally known only by the web server. If it matches, you're in. This isn't safe if your API site is exposed to the public with HTTP instead of HTTPS. If it's hidden behind a frontend site that is itself open, the frontends and backends could communicate using a shared constant secret. But if your frontend site is hacked, then darn. Let's see how FastAPI handles simple authentication.

Make a new top-level file called *auth.py*. Check that you don't have another FastAPI server still running from one of those ever-changing *main.py* files from previous chapters. Example 11-1 implements a server that just returns whatever username and password were sent to it using HTTP Basic Authentication—a method from the original days of the web.

Example 11-1. Use HTTP Basic Auth to get user info: auth.py

```
import uvicorn
from fastapi import Depends, FastAPI
from fastapi.security import HTTPBasic, HTTPBasicCredentials

app = FastAPI()

basic = HTTPBasic()

@app.get("/who")
def get_user(
```

```
    creds: HTTPBasicCredentials = Depends(basic)):
    return {"username": creds.username, "password": creds.password}

if __name__ == "__main__":
    uvicorn.run("auth:app", reload=True)
```

In Example 11-2, tell HTTPie to make this Basic Auth request (this requires the arguments -a *name:password*). Here, let's use the name me and the password secret.

Example 11-2. Test with HTTPie

```
$ http -q -a me:secret localhost:8000/who
{
    "password": "secret",
    "username": "me"
}
```

Testing with the Requests package in Example 11-3 is similar, using the auth
parameter.

Example 11-3. Test with Requests

```
>>> import requests
>>> r = requests.get("http://localhost:8000/who",
    auth=("me", "secret"))
>>> r.json()
{'username': 'me', 'password': 'secret'}
```

You can also test Example 11-1 with the automatic docs page (*http://localhost:8000/
docs*), shown in Figure 11-1.

Figure 11-1. Docs page for simple authentication

Click that down arrow on the right, then the Try It Out button, and then the Execute button. You'll see a form requesting the username and password. Type anything. The documentation form will hit that server endpoint and show those values in the response.

These tests show that you can get a username and password to the server and back (although none of these actually checked anything). Something in the server needs to verify that this name and password match the approved values. So, in Example 11-4, I'll include a single secret username and password in the web server. The username and password that you pass in now needs to match them (each is a *shared secret*), or you'll get an exception. The HTTP status code 401 is officially called Unauthorized, but it really means *unauthenticated*.

 Instead of memorizing all the HTTP status codes, you can import FastAPI's status module (which itself is imported directly from Starlette). So you can use the more explanatory status_code= HTTP_401_UNAUTHORIZED in Example 11-4 instead of a plain status_code=401.

Example 11-4. Add a secret username and password to auth.py

```
import uvicorn
from fastapi import Depends, FastAPI, HTTPException
from fastapi.security import HTTPBasic, HTTPBasicCredentials

app = FastAPI()

secret_user: str = "newphone"
secret_password: str = "whodis?"

basic: HTTPBasicCredentials = HTTPBasic()

@app.get("/who")
def get_user(
    creds: HTTPBasicCredentials = Depends(basic)) -> dict:
    if (creds.username == secret_user and
        creds.password == secret_password):
        return {"username": creds.username,
            "password": creds.password}
    raise HTTPException(status_code=401, detail="Hey!")

if __name__ == "__main__":
    uvicorn.run("auth:app", reload=True)
```

Misguessing the username and password will earn a mild 401 rebuke in Example 11-5.

Example 11-5. Test with HTTPie and a mismatched username/password

```
$ http -a me:secret localhost:8000/who
HTTP/1.1 401 Unauthorized
content-length: 17
content-type: application/json
date: Fri, 03 Mar 2023 03:25:09 GMT
server: uvicorn

{
    "detail": "Hey!"
}
```

Using the magic combination returns the username and password, as before, in Example 11-6.

Example 11-6. Test with HTTPie and the correct username/password

```
$ http -q -a newphone:whodis? localhost:8000/who
{
    "password": "whodis?",
    "username": "newphone"
}
```

Simple Individual Authentication

The previous section showed how you could use a shared secret to control access. It's a broad approach, not very secure. And it doesn't tell you anything about the individual visitor, just that they (or a sentient AI) know the secret.

Many websites want to do the following:

- Define individual visitors in some way
- Identify specific visitors as they access certain endpoints (authentication)
- Possibly assign different permissions to some visitors and endpoints (authorization)
- Possibly save specific information per visitor (interests, purchases, and so on)

If your visitors are humans, you may want them to provide a username or email and a password. If they're external programs, you may want them to provide an API key and secret.

From here on, I'll use just *username* to refer to either a user-selected name or an email.

To authenticate real individual users instead of a fake one, you'll need to do a bit more:

- Pass the user values (name and password) to the API server endpoints as HTTP headers.
- Use HTTPS instead of HTTP, to avoid anyone snooping the text of these headers.
- *Hash* the password to a different string. The result is not "de-hashable"—you can't derive the original password from its hash.
- Make a real database store a User database table containing the username and the hashed password (never the original plain-text password).
- Hash the newly input password and compare the result with the hashed password in the database.
- If the username and hashed password match, pass the matching User object up the stack. If they don't match, return None or raise an exception.
- In the Service layer, fire off any metrics/logging/whatever that are relevant to individual user authentication.
- In the Web layer, send the authenticated user info to any functions that require it.

I'll show you how to do all these things in the following sections, using recent tools like OAuth2 and JWT.

Fancier Individual Authentication

If you want to authenticate individuals, you have to store some individual information somewhere—for example, in a database containing records with at least a key (username or API key), and a secret (password or API secret). Your website visitors will provide these when accessing protected URLs, and you need something in the database to match them with.

The official FastAPI security docs (introductory (*https://oreil.ly/kkTUB*) and advanced (*https://oreil.ly/biKwy*)) have top-down descriptions of how to set up authentication for multiple users, using a local database. But, example web functions fake the actual database access.

Here, you'll do the opposite: starting at the Data layer and working up. You'll define how a user/visitor is defined, stored, and accessed. Then you'll work up to the Web layer, and how user identification is passed in, evaluated, and authenticated.

OAuth2

> OAuth 2.0, which stands for "Open Authorization," is a standard designed to allow a website or application to access resources hosted by other web apps on behalf of a user.
>
> —Auth0

In the early trusting web days, you could provide your login name and password of a website (let's call it B) to another website (A, of course) and let it access stuff on B for you. This would give A *full access* to B, although it was trusted to access only what it was supposed to. Examples of B and resources were things like Twitter followers, Facebook friends, email contacts, and so on. Of course, this couldn't last long, so various companies and groups got together to define OAuth. It was originally designed only to allow website A to access specific (not all) resources on website B.

OAuth2 (*https://oauth.net/2*) is a popular but complex *authorization* standard, with uses beyond the A/B example. There are many explanations of it, from light (*https:// oreil.ly/ehmuf*) to heavy (*https://oreil.ly/qAUaM*).

There used to be an OAuth1 (*https://oauth.net/1*), but it isn't used anymore. Some of the original OAuth2 recommendations are now deprecated (computerese for *don't use them*). On the horizon are OAuth2.1 (*https://oauth.net/2.1*) and, even further into the mist, txauth (*https://oreil.ly/5PW2T*).

OAuth offers various flows (*https://oreil.ly/kRiWh*) for different circumstances. I'll use the *authorization code flow* here. This section will walk through an implementation, one average-sized step at a time.

First, you'll need to install these third-party Python packages:

JWT handling
```
pip install python-jose[cryptography]
```

Secure password handling
```
pip install passlib
```

Form handling
```
pip install python-multipart
```

The following sections start with the user data model and database management, and work up the familiar layers to the Service and Web, where OAuth pops up.

User Model

Let's start with the very minimal user model definitions in Example 11-7. These will be used in all layers.

Example 11-7. User definition: model/user.py

```
from pydantic import BaseModel

class User(BaseModel):
    name: str
    hash: str
```

A User object contains an arbitrary name plus a hash string (the hashed password, not the original plain-text password), and is what's saved in the database. We'll need both to authenticate a visitor.

User Data Layer

Example 11-8 contains the user database code.

 The code creates user (active users) and xuser (deleted users) tables. Often developers add a Boolean deleted field to a user table to indicate the user is no longer active, without actually deleting the record from the table. I prefer moving the deleted user's data to another table. This avoids repetitive checking of the deleted field in all user queries. It can also help speed up queries: making an index for a *low cardinality* field like a Boolean does no good.

Example 11-8. Data layer: data/user.py

```
from model.user import User
from .init import (conn, curs, get_db, IntegrityError)
from error import Missing, Duplicate

curs.execute("""create table if not exists
                user(
                  name text primary key,
                  hash text)""")
curs.execute("""create table if not exists
                xuser(
                  name text primary key,
                  hash text)""")

def row_to_model(row: tuple) -> User:
    name, hash = row
    return User(name=name, hash=hash)
```

```python
def model_to_dict(user: User) -> dict:
    return user.dict()

def get_one(name: str) -> User:
    qry = "select * from user where name=:name"
    params = {"name": name}
    curs.execute(qry, params)
    row = curs.fetchone()
    if row:
        return row_to_model(row)
    else:
        raise Missing(msg=f"User {name} not found")

def get_all() -> list[User]:
    qry = "select * from user"
    curs.execute(qry)
    return [row_to_model(row) for row in curs.fetchall()]

def create(user: User, table:str = "user"):
    """Add <user> to user or xuser table"""
    qry = f"""insert into {table}
        (name, hash)
        values
        (:name, :hash)"""
    params = model_to_dict(user)
    try:
        curs.execute(qry, params)
    except IntegrityError:
        raise Duplicate(msg=
            f"{table}: user {user.name} already exists")

def modify(name: str, user: User)  -> User:
    qry = """update user set
            name=:name, hash=:hash
            where name=:name0"""
    params = {
        "name": user.name,
        "hash": user.hash,
        "name0": name}
    curs.execute(qry, params)
    if curs.rowcount == 1:
        return get_one(user.name)
    else:
        raise Missing(msg=f"User {name} not found")

def delete(name: str) -> None:
    """Drop user with <name> from user table, add to xuser table"""
    user = get_one(name)
    qry = "delete from user where name = :name"
    params = {"name": name}
    curs.execute(qry, params)
    if curs.rowcount != 1:
```

```
        raise Missing(msg=f"User {name} not found")
    create(user, table="xuser")
```

User Fake Data Layer

The module in Example 11-9 is used in tests that exclude the database but need some
user data.

Example 11-9. Fake layer: fake/user.py

```
from model.user import User
from error import Missing, Duplicate

# (no hashed password checking in this module)
fakes = [
    User(name="kwijobo",
        hash="abc"),
    User(name="ermagerd",
        hash="xyz"),
    ]

def find(name: str) -> User | None:
    for e in fakes:
        if e.name == name:
            return e
    return None

def check_missing(name: str):
    if not find(name):
        raise Missing(msg=f"Missing user {name}")

def check_duplicate(name: str):
    if find(name):
        raise Duplicate(msg=f"Duplicate user {name}")

def get_all() -> list[User]:
    """Return all users"""
    return fakes

def get_one(name: str) -> User:
    """Return one user"""
    check_missing(name)
    return find(name)

def create(user: User) -> User:
    """Add a user"""
    check_duplicate(user.name)
    return user

def modify(name: str, user: User) -> User:
    """Partially modify a user"""
```

```
    check_missing(name)
    return user

def delete(name: str) -> None:
    """Delete a user"""
    check_missing(name)
    return None
```

User Service Layer

Example 11-10 defines the Service layer for users. A difference from the other Service layer modules is the addition of OAuth2 and JWT functions. I think it's cleaner to have them here than in the Web layer, though a few OAuth2 Web-layer functions are in the upcoming *web/user.py*.

The CRUD functions are still pass-throughs for now but could be flavored to taste with metrics in the future. Notice that, like the creature and explorer services, this design supports runtime use of either the fake or real Data layers to access user data.

Example 11-10. Service layer: service/user.py

```
from datetime import timedelta, datetime
import os
from jose import jwt
from model.user import User

if os.getenv("CRYPTID_UNIT_TEST"):
    from fake import user as data
else:
    from data import user as data

# --- New auth stuff

from passlib.context import CryptContext

# Change SECRET_KEY for production!
SECRET_KEY = "keep-it-secret-keep-it-safe"
ALGORITHM = "HS256"
pwd_context = CryptContext(schemes=["bcrypt"], deprecated="auto")

def verify_password(plain: str, hash: str) -> bool:
    """Hash <plain> and compare with <hash> from the database"""
    return pwd_context.verify(plain, hash)

def get_hash(plain: str) -> str:
    """Return the hash of a <plain> string"""
    return pwd_context.hash(plain)

def get_jwt_username(token:str) -> str | None:
    """Return username from JWT access <token>"""
```

```python
    try:
        payload = jwt.decode(token, SECRET_KEY, algorithms=[ALGORITHM])
        if not (username := payload.get("sub")):
            return None
    except jwt.JWTError:
        return None
    return username

def get_current_user(token: str) -> User | None:
    """Decode an OAuth access <token> and return the User"""
    if not (username := get_jwt_username(token)):
        return None
    if (user := lookup_user(username)):
        return user
    return None

def lookup_user(username: str) -> User | None:
    """Return a matching User from the database for <name>"""
    if (user := data.get(username)):
        return user
    return None

def auth_user(name: str, plain: str) -> User | None:
    """Authenticate user <name> and <plain> password"""
    if not (user := lookup_user(name)):
        return None
    if not verify_password(plain, user.hash):
        return None
    return user

def create_access_token(data: dict,
    expires: timedelta | None = None
):
    """Return a JWT access token"""
    src = data.copy()
    now = datetime.utcnow()
    if not expires:
        expires = timedelta(minutes=15)
    src.update({"exp": now + expires})
    encoded_jwt = jwt.encode(src, SECRET_KEY, algorithm=ALGORITHM)
    return encoded_jwt

# --- CRUD passthrough stuff

def get_all() -> list[User]:
    return data.get_all()

def get_one(name) -> User:
    return data.get_one(name)

def create(user: User) -> User:
    return data.create(user)
```

```
def modify(name: str, user: User) -> User:
    return data.modify(name, user)

def delete(name: str) -> None:
    return data.delete(name)
```

User Web Layer

Example 11-11 defines the base user module in the Web layer. It uses the new auth code from the *service/user.py* module in Example 11-10.

Example 11-11. Web layer: web/user.py

```
import os
from fastapi import APIRouter, HTTPException
from fastapi.security import OAuth2PasswordBearer, OAuth2PasswordRequestForm
from model.user import User
if os.getenv("CRYPTID_UNIT_TEST"):
    from fake import user as service
else:
    from service import user as service
from error import Missing, Duplicate

ACCESS_TOKEN_EXPIRE_MINUTES = 30

router = APIRouter(prefix = "/user")

# --- new auth stuff

# This dependency makes a post to "/user/token"
# (from a form containing a username and password)
# and returns an access token.
oauth2_dep = OAuth2PasswordBearer(tokenUrl="token")

def unauthed():
    raise HTTPException(
        status_code=401,
        detail="Incorrect username or password",
        headers={"WWW-Authenticate": "Bearer"},
        )

# This endpoint is directed to by any call that has the
# oauth2_dep() dependency:
@router.post("/token")
async def create_access_token(
    form_data: OAuth2PasswordRequestForm = Depends()
):
    """Get username and password from OAuth form,
        return access token"""
    user = service.auth_user(form_data.username, form_data.password)
```

```python
    if not user:
        unauthed()
    expires = timedelta(minutes=ACCESS_TOKEN_EXPIRE_MINUTES)
    access_token = service.create_access_token(
        data={"sub": user.username}, expires=expires
    )
    return {"access_token": access_token, "token_type": "bearer"}

@app.get("/token")
def get_access_token(token: str = Depends(oauth2_dep)) -> dict:
    """Return the current access token"""
    return {"token": token}

# --- previous CRUD stuff

@router.get("/")
def get_all() -> list[User]:
    return service.get_all()

@router.get("/{name}")
def get_one(name) -> User:
    try:
        return service.get_one(name)
    except Missing as exc:
        raise HTTPException(status_code=404, detail=exc.msg)

@router.post("/", status_code=201)
def create(user: User) -> User:
    try:
        return service.create(user)
    except Duplicate as exc:
        raise HTTPException(status_code=409, detail=exc.msg)

@router.patch("/")
def modify(name: str, user: User) -> User:
    try:
        return service.modify(name, user)
    except Missing as exc:
        raise HTTPException(status_code=404, detail=exc.msg)

@router.delete("/{name}")
def delete(name: str) -> None:
    try:
        return service.delete(name)
    except Missing as exc:
        raise HTTPException(status_code=404, detail=exc.msg)
```

Test!

The unit and full tests for this new user component are similar to those that you've already seen for creatures and explorers. Rather than using the ink and paper here, you can view them at this book's accompanying website.[1]

Top Layer

The previous section defined a new `router` variable for URLs starting with */user*, so Example 11-12 adds this subrouter.

Example 11-12. Top layer: main.py

```python
from fastapi import FastAPI
from web import explorer, creature, user

app = FastAPI()
app.include_router(explorer.router)
app.include_router(creature.router)
app.include_router(user.router)
```

When Uvicorn autoreloads, the */user/...* endpoints should now be available.

That was fun, in a stretched definition of fun. Given all the user code that was just created, let's give it something to do.

Authentication Steps

Here's a review of that heap of code from the previous sections:

- If an endpoint has the dependency `oauth2_dep()` (in *web/user.py*), a form containing username and password fields is generated and sent to the client.
- After the client fills out and submits this form, the username and password (hashed with the same algorithm as those already stored in the local database) are matched against the local database.
- If a match occurs, an access token is generated (in JWT format) and returned.
- This access token is passed back to the web server as an `Authorization` HTTP header in subsequent requests. This JWT token is decoded on the local server to the username and other details. This name does not need to be looked up in the database again.
- The username is authenticated, and the server can do whatever it likes with it.

---

1 If I were paid by the line, fate might have intervened.

What can the server do with this hard-won authentication information? The server can do the following:

- Generate metrics (this user, this endpoint, this time) to help study what's being viewed, by whom, for how long, and so on.
- Save user-specific information.

JWT

This section contains some details on the JWT. You really don't need them to use all the earlier code in this chapter, but if you're a little curious…

A JWT (*https://jwt.io*) is an encoding scheme, not an authentication method. The low-level details are defined in RFC 7519 (*https://oreil.ly/_op1j*). It can be used to convey authentication information for OAuth2 (and other methods), and I'll show that here.

A JWT is a readable string with three dot-separated sections:

- *Header*: Encryption algorithm used, and token type
- *Payload*: …
- *Signature*: …

Each section consists of a JSON string, encoded in Base 64 URL (*https://www.base64url.com*) format. Here's an example (which has been split at the dots to fit on this page):

```
eyJhbGciOiJIUzI1NiIsInR5cCI6IkpXVCJ9.
eyJzdWIiOiIxMjM0NTY3ODkwIiwibmFtZSI6IkpvaG4gRG9lIiwiaWF0IjoxNTE2MjM5MDIyfQ.
SflKxwRJSMeKKF2QT4fwpMeJf36POk6yJV_adQssw5c
```

As a plain ASCII string that's also safe to use in URLs, it can be passed to web servers as part of the URL, a query parameter, HTTP header, cookie, and so on.

JWT avoids a database lookup, but this also means that you can't detect a revoked authorization directly.

Third-Party Authentication: OIDC

You'll often see websites that let you log in with an ID and password, or let you log in via your account at a different site, like Google, Facebook/Meta, LinkedIn, or many others. These frequently use a standard called OpenID Connect (OIDC) (*https://openid.net/connect*), which is built atop OAuth2. When you connect to an external OIDC-enabled site, you'll get back an OAuth2 access token (as in the examples in this chapter), but also an *ID token*.

The official FastAPI docs don't include example code for integration with OIDC. If you want to try it, some third-party packages (FastAPI-specific and more generic) will save time over rolling your own implementation:

- FastAPI OIDC (*https://oreil.ly/TDABr*)
- fastapi-third-party-auth (*https://oreil.ly/yGaO6*)
- FastAPI Resource Server (*https://oreil.ly/THByF*)
- oauthlib (*https://oreil.ly/J-pDB*)
- oic (*https://oreil.ly/AgYKZ*)
- OIDC Client (*https://oreil.ly/e9QGb*)
- oidc-op (*https://oreil.ly/cJCF4*)
- OpenID Connect (*https://oreil.ly/WH49I*)

The FastAPI Repo Issues page (*https://oreil.ly/ztR3r*) includes multiple code examples, and a comment from tiangelo (Sebastián Ramírez) that FastAPI OIDC examples will be included in the official docs and tutorials in the future.

Authorization

Authentication handles the *who* (identity), and authorization handles the *what*: which resources (web endpoints) are you allowed to access, and in what way? The number of combinations of *who* and *what* can be large.

In this book, explorers and creatures have been the main resources. Looking up an explorer, or listing all of them, would typically be more "open" than adding or modifying an existing one. If the website is supposed to be a reliable interface to some data, write access should be more limited than read access. Because, grr, people.

If every endpoint is completely open, you don't need authorization and can skip this section. The simplest authorization could be a simple Boolean (is this user an admin or not?); for the examples in this book, you might require admin authorization to add, delete, or modify an explorer or creature. If your database has lots of entries, you might also want to limit the get_all() functions with further permissions for non-admins. As the website gets more complex, the permissions might become more fine-grained.

Let's look at a progression of authorization cases. We'll use the User table, in which the name can be an email, username, or API key; "pair" tables are the relational database way of matching entries from two separate tables:

- If you want to track only admin visitors and leave the rest anonymous:
  — Use an `Admin` table of authenticated usernames. You'd look up the name from the `Admin` table, and if matched, compare the hashed passwords from the `User` table.
- If *all* visitors should be authenticated, but you need to authorize admins for only some endpoints:
  — Authenticate everyone as in the earlier examples (from the `User` table), and then check the `Admin` table to see if this user is also an admin.
- For more than one type of permission (such as read-only, read, write):
  — Use a `Permission` definition table.
  — Use a `UserPermission` table that pairs users and permissions. This is sometimes called an *access control list*.
- If permission combinations are complex, add a level and define *roles* (independent sets of permissions):
  — Create a `Role` table.
  — Create a `UserRole` table pairing `User` and `Role` entries. This is sometimes called *role-based access control* (RBAC).

Middleware

FastAPI enables insertion of code at the Web layer that does the following:

- Intercepts the request
- Does something with the request
- Passes the request to a path function
- Intercepts the response returned by the patch function
- Does something with the response
- Returns the response to the caller

It's similar to what a Python decorator does to the function that it "wraps."

In some cases, you could use either middleware or dependency injection with `Depends()`. Middleware is handier for more global security issues like CORS, which brings up…

CORS

Cross-origin resource sharing (CORS) involves communication between other trusted servers and your website. If your site has all the frontend and backend code in one place, then there's no problem. But these days, it's common to have a JavaScript frontend talking to a backend written in something like FastAPI. These servers will not have the same *origin*:

Protocol
    `http` or `https`

Domain
    Internet domain, like `google.com` or `localhost`

Port
    Numeric TCP/IP port on that domain, like `80`, `443`, or `8000`

How does the backend know a trustable frontend from a box of moldy radishes, or a mustache-twirling attacker? That's a job for CORS, which specifies what the backend trusts, the most prominent being the following:

- Origins
- HTTP methods
- HTTP headers
- CORS cache timeout

You hook into CORS at the Web level. Example 11-13 shows how to allow only one frontend server (with the domain *https://ui.cryptids.com*), and any HTTP headers or methods.

Example 11-13. Activate the CORS middleware

```
from fastapi import FastAPI, Request
from fastapi.middleware.cors import CORSMiddleware

app = FastAPI()

app.add_middleware(
    CORSMiddleware,
    allow_origins=["https://ui.cryptids.com",],
    allow_credentials=True,
    allow_methods=["*"],
    allow_headers=["*"],
    )

@app.get("/test_cors")
```

```
def test_cors(request: Request):
    print(request)
```

Once that's done, any other domain that tries to contact your backend site directly will be refused.

Third-Party Packages

You've now read examples of how to code authentication and authorization solutions with FastAPI. But maybe you don't need to do everything yourself. The FastAPI ecosystem is growing fast, and packages may be available that do a lot of the work for you.

Here are some untested examples. There are no guarantees that any package in this list will still be around and supported over time, but they may be worth a look:

- FastAPI Users (*https://oreil.ly/ueVfq*)
- FastAPI JWT Auth (*https://oreil.ly/ooGSK*)
- FastAPI-Login (*https://oreil.ly/oWA3p*)
- fastapi-auth0 (*https://oreil.ly/fHfkU*)
- AuthX (*https://authx.yezz.me*)
- FastAPI-User-Auth (*https://oreil.ly/J57xu*)
- fastapi-authz (*https://oreil.ly/aAGzW*)
- fastapi-opa (*https://oreil.ly/Bvzv3*)
- FastAPI-key-auth (*https://oreil.ly/s-Ui5*)
- FastAPI Auth Middleware (*https://oreil.ly/jnR-s*)
- fastapi-jwt (*https://oreil.ly/RrxUZ*)
- fastapi_auth2 (*https://oreil.ly/5DXkB*)
- fastapi-sso (*https://oreil.ly/GLTdt*)
- Fief (*https://www.fief.dev*)

Review

This was a heavier chapter than most. It showed ways that you can authenticate visitors and authorize them to do certain things. These are two aspects of web security. The chapter also discussed CORS, another important web security topic.

## CHAPTER 12

Testing

A QA engineer walks into a bar. Orders a beer. Orders 0 beers. Orders 99999999999 beers. Orders a lizard. Orders −1 beers. Orders a ueicbksjdhd.

First real customer walks in and asks where the bathroom is. The bar bursts into flames, killing everyone.

—Brenan Keller, Twitter

Preview

This chapter discusses the kinds of testing that you would perform on a FastAPI site: *unit*, *integration*, and *full*. It features *pytest* and automated test development.

Web API Testing

You've already seen several manual API testing tools as endpoints have been added:

- HTTPie
- Requests
- HTTPX
- The web browser

And many more testing tools are available:

- Curl (*https://curl.se*) is very well known, although in this book I've used HTTPie instead for its simpler syntax.
- Httpbin (*http://httpbin.org*), written by the author of Requests, is a free test server that provides many views into your HTTP request.

- Postman (*https://www.postman.com*) is a full API test platform.
- Chrome DevTools (*https://oreil.ly/eUK_R*) is a rich toolset, part of the Chrome browser.

These can all be used for full (end-to-end) tests, such as those you've seen in the previous chapters. Those manual tests have been useful for quickly verifying code just after it's typed.

But what if a change that you make later breaks one of those earlier manual tests (a *regression*)? You don't want to rerun dozens of tests after every code change. That's when *automated* tests become important. The rest of this chapter focuses on these, and how to build them with pytest.

Where to Test

I've mentioned the varieties of tests:

Unit
> Within a layer, tests individual functions

Integration
> Across layers, tests connectivity

Full
> Tests the full API and stack beneath it

Sometimes these are called a *test pyramid*, with the width indicating the relative number of tests that should be in each group (Figure 12-1).

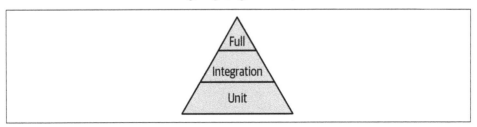

Figure 12-1. Test pyramid

What to Test

What should you test as you're writing code? Basically, for a given input, confirm that you get the correct output. You might check the following:

- Missing inputs
- Duplicate inputs

- Incorrect input types
- Incorrect input order
- Invalid input values
- Huge inputs or outputs

Errors can happen anywhere:

The Web layer
Pydantic will catch any mismatch with the model and return a 422 HTTP status code.

The Data layer
The database will raise exceptions for missing or duplicate data, as well as SQL query syntax errors. Timeouts or memory exhaustion may occur when passing a huge data result in one piece, instead of in chunks with a generator or pagination.

Any layer
Plain old bugs and oversights can occur.

Chapters 8 through 10 contained some of these tests:

- *Full manual tests*, using tools like HTTPie
- *Unit manual tests*, as Python fragments
- *Automated tests*, using pytest scripts

The next few sections expand on pytest.

Pytest

Python has long had the standard package unittest (*https://oreil.ly/3u0M_*). A later third-party package called nose (*https://nose.readthedocs.io*) tried to improve on it. Most Python developers now prefer pytest (*https://docs.pytest.org*), which does more than either of these and is easier to use. It isn't built into Python, so you'll need to run `pip install pytest` if you don't already have it. Also, run `pip install pytest-mock` to get the automatic `mocker` fixture; you'll see this later in this chapter.

What does pytest offer? Nice automatic features include the following:

Test discovery
A test prefix or test suffix in a Python filename will be run automatically. This filename matching goes down into subdirectories, executing as many tests as you have there.

Assertion failure details
A failing `assert` statement prints what was expected and what actually happened.

Fixtures
These functions can run once for the whole test script, or run for every test (its *scope*), providing test functions with parameters like standard test data or database initialization. Fixtures are a sort of dependency injection, like FastAPI offers for web path functions: specific data passed to a general test function.

Parameterization
This provides multiple test data to a test function.

Layout

Where should you put your tests? There doesn't seem to be wide agreement, but here are two reasonable designs:

- A *test* directory at the top, with subdirectories for the code area being tested (like *web*, *service*, etc.)
- A *test* directory under each code directory (like *web*, *service*, etc.).

Also, within the specific subdirectory like *test/web*, should you make more directories for different test types (like *unit*, *integration*, and *full*)? In this book, I'm using this hierarchy:

```
test
├── unit
│   ├── web
│   ├── service
│   └── data
├── integration
└── full
```

Individual test scripts live within the bottom directories. Those are in this chapter.

Automated Unit Tests

A unit test should check one thing, within one layer. This usually means passing parameter(s) to a function and asserting what should be returned.

Unit tests require *isolation* of the code being tested. If not, you're also testing something else. So, how do you isolate code for unit tests?

Mocking

In this book's code stack, accessing a URL via a web API generally calls a function in the Web layer, which calls a function in the Service layer, which calls a function in the

Data layer, which accesses a database. The results flow back up the chain, eventually back out of the Web layer to the caller.

Unit testing sounds simple. For each function in your codebase, pass in test arguments and confirm that it returns expected values. This works well for a *pure function*: one that takes input arguments and returns responses without referencing any external code. But most functions also call other functions, so how can you control what those other functions do? What about the data that comes from these external sources? The most common external factor to control is database access, but really it can be anything.

One method is to *mock* each external function call. Because functions are first-class objects in Python, you can substitute one function for another. The unittest package has a mock module that does this.

Many developers believe that mocking is the best way to isolate unit tests. I'll first show examples of mocking here, along with the argument that often mocking requires too much knowledge of *how* your code works, rather than the results. You may hear the terms *structural testing* (as in mocks, where the tested code is quite visible) and *behavioral testing* (where the code internals are not needed).

Examples 12-1 and 12-2 define the modules *mod1.py* and *mod2.py*.

Example 12-1. Called module (mod1.py)

```
def preamble() -> str:
    return "The sum is "
```

Example 12-2. Calling module (mod2.py)

```
import mod1

def summer(x: int, y:int) -> str:
    return mod1.preamble() + f"{x+y}"
```

The summer() function calculates the sum of its arguments, and returns a string with a preamble and the sum. Example 12-3 is a minimal pytest script to verify summer().

Example 12-3. Pytest script test_summer1.py

```
import mod2

def test_summer():
    assert "The sum is 11" == mod2.summer(5,6)
```

Example 12-4 runs the test successfully.

Example 12-4. Run the pytest script

```
$ pytest -q test_summer1.py
.                                                          [100%]
1 passed in 0.04s
```

(The -q runs the test quietly, without lots of extra printed details.) OK, it passed. But the summer() function got some text from the preamble function. What if we just want to test that the addition succeeded?

We could write a new function that just returns the stringified sum of two numbers, and then rewrite summer() to return this appended to the preamble() string.

Or, we could mock preamble() to remove its effect, as shown in multiple ways in Example 12-5.

Example 12-5. Pytest with a mock (test_summer2.py)

```python
from unittest import mock
import mod1
import mod2

def test_summer_a():
    with mock.patch("mod1.preamble", return_value=""):
        assert "11" == mod2.summer(5,6)

def test_summer_b():
    with mock.patch("mod1.preamble") as mock_preamble:
        mock_preamble.return_value=""
        assert "11" == mod2.summer(5,6)

@mock.patch("mod1.preamble", return_value="")
def test_summer_c(mock_preamble):
    assert "11" == mod2.summer(5,6)

@mock.patch("mod1.preamble")
def test_caller_d(mock_preamble):
    mock_preamble.return_value = ""
    assert "11" == mod2.summer(5,6)
```

These tests show that mocks can be created in more than one way. The function test_caller_a() uses mock.patch() as a Python *context manager* (the with statement). Its arguments are listed here:

"mod1.preamble"
: The full string name of the preamble() function in module mod1.

return_value=""
: Makes this mocked version return an empty string.

The test_caller_b() function is almost the same, but adds as mock_preamble to use the mock object on the next line.

The test_caller_c() function defines the mock with a Python *decorator*. The mocked object is passed as an argument to test_caller2().

The test_caller_d() function is like test_caller_b(), setting the return_value in a separate call to mock_preamble.

In each case, the string name of the thing to be mocked must match the way it's called in the code that's being tested—in this case, summer(). The mock library converts this string name to a variable that will intercept any references to the original variable with that name. (Remember that in Python, variables are just references to the real objects.)

So, when Example 12-6 is run, in all four summer() test functions, when summer(5,6) is called, the changeling mock preamble() is called instead of the real one. The mocked version drops that string, so the test can ensure that summer() returns a string version of the sum of its two arguments.

Example 12-6. Run mocked pytest

```
$ pytest -q test_summer2.py
....                                                    [100%]
4 passed in 0.13s
```

 That was a contrived case, for simplicity. Mocking can be quite complex; see articles like "Understanding the Python Mock Object Library" by Alex Ronquillo (*https://oreil.ly/I0bkd*) for clear examples, and the official Python docs (*https://oreil.ly/hN9lZ*) for the harrowing details.

Test Doubles and Fakes

To perform that mock, you needed to know that the summer() function imported the function preamble() from the module mod1. This was a structural test, requiring knowledge of specific variable and module names.

Is there a way to perform a behavioral test that doesn't need this?

One way is to define a *double*: separate code that does what we want in the test—in this case, make preamble() return an empty string. One way to do this is with imports. Apply this to this example first, before using it for unit tests in the layers of the next three sections.

First, redefine *mod2.py* in Example 12-7.

Example 12-7. Make mod2.py *import a double if unit testing*

```
import os
if os.get_env("UNIT_TEST"):
    import fake_mod1 as mod1
else:
    import mod1

def summer(x: int, y:int) -> str:
    return mod1.preamble() + f"{x+y}"
```

Example 12-8 defines that double module *fake_mod1.py*.

Example 12-8. Double fake_mod1.py

```
def preamble() -> str:
    return ""
```

And Example 12-9 is the test.

Example 12-9. Test script test_summer_fake.py

```
import os
os.environ["UNIT_TEST"] = "true"
import mod2

def test_summer_fake():
    assert "11" == mod2.summer(5,6)
```

....which Example 12-10 runs.

Example 12-10. Run the new unit test

```
$ pytest -q test_summer_fake.py
.                                                        [100%]
1 passed in 0.04s
```

This import-switching method does require adding a check for an environment variable, but avoids having to write specific mocks for function calls. You can be the judge of which you prefer. The next few sections will use the import method, which works nicely with the *fake* package that I'd been using as I defined the code layers.

To summarize, these examples replaced preamble() with a *mock* in a test script or imported a doppelgänger *double*. You can isolate the code being tested in other ways, but these work and are not as tricky as others that Google might find for you.

Web

This layer implements the site's API. Ideally, each path function (endpoint) should have at least one test—maybe more, if the function could fail in more than one way. At the Web layer, you typically want to see if the endpoint exists, works with the correct parameters, and returns the right status code and data.

 These are shallow API tests, testing solely within the Web layer. So, Service-layer calls (which would in turn call the Data layer and the database) need to be intercepted, along with any other calls that exit the Web layer.

Using the `import` idea of the previous section, use the environment variable CRYP TID_UNIT_TEST to import the *fake* package as `service`, instead of the real `service`. This stops Web functions from calling Service functions, and instead short-circuits them to the *fake* (doubles) version. Then the lower Data layer and database aren't involved, either. We get what we want: unit tests. Example 12-11 has the modified *web/creature.py* file.

Example 12-11. Modified web/creature.py

```python
import os
from fastapi import APIRouter, HTTPException
from model.creature import Creature
if os.getenv("CRYPTID_UNIT_TEST"):
    from fake import creature as service
else:
    from service import creature as service
from error import Missing, Duplicate

router = APIRouter(prefix = "/creature")

@router.get("/")
def get_all() -> list[Creature]:
    return service.get_all()

@router.get("/{name}")
def get_one(name) -> Creature:
    try:
        return service.get_one(name)
    except Missing as exc:
        raise HTTPException(status_code=404, detail=exc.msg)

@router.post("/", status_code=201)
def create(creature: Creature) -> Creature:
    try:
        return service.create(creature)
```

```
        except Duplicate as exc:
            raise HTTPException(status_code=409, detail=exc.msg)

@router.patch("/")
def modify(name: str, creature: Creature) -> Creature:
    try:
        return service.modify(name, creature)
    except Missing as exc:
        raise HTTPException(status_code=404, detail=exc.msg)


@router.delete("/{name}")
def delete(name: str) -> None:
    try:
        return service.delete(name)
    except Missing as exc:
        raise HTTPException(status_code=404, detail=exc.msg)
```

Example 12-12 has tests, using two pytest fixtures:

sample()
> A new Creature object

fakes()
> A list of "existing" creatures

The fakes are obtained from a lower-level module. By setting the environment variable CRYPTID_UNIT_TEST, the Web module from Example 12-11 imports the fake service version (providing fake data rather than calling the database) instead of the real one. This isolates the tests, which is the point.

Example 12-12. Web unit tests for creatures, using fixtures

```
from fastapi import HTTPException
import pytest
import os
os.environ["CRYPTID_UNIT_TEST"] = "true"
from model.creature import Creature
from web import creature

@pytest.fixture
def sample() -> Creature:
    return Creature(name="dragon",
        description="Wings! Fire! Aieee!",
        country="*")

@pytest.fixture
def fakes() -> list[Creature]:
    return creature.get_all()
```

```
def assert_duplicate(exc):
    assert exc.value.status_code == 404
    assert "Duplicate" in exc.value.msg

def assert_missing(exc):
    assert exc.value.status_code == 404
    assert "Missing" in exc.value.msg

def test_create(sample):
    assert creature.create(sample) == sample

def test_create_duplicate(fakes):
    with pytest.raises(HTTPException) as exc:
        _ = creature.create(fakes[0])
        assert_duplicate(exc)

def test_get_one(fakes):
    assert creature.get_one(fakes[0].name) == fakes[0]

def test_get_one_missing():
    with pytest.raises(HTTPException) as exc:
        _ = creature.get_one("bobcat")
        assert_missing(exc)

def test_modify(fakes):
    assert creature.modify(fakes[0].name, fakes[0]) == fakes[0]

def test_modify_missing(sample):
    with pytest.raises(HTTPException) as exc:
        _ = creature.modify(sample.name, sample)
        assert_missing(exc)

def test_delete(fakes):
    assert creature.delete(fakes[0].name) is None

def test_delete_missing(sample):
    with pytest.raises(HTTPException) as exc:
        _ = creature.delete("emu")
        assert_missing(exc)
```

Service

In a way, the Service layer is the important one and could be connected to different Web and Data layers. Example 12-13 is similar to Example 12-11, differing mainly in the import and use of the lower-level data module. It also doesn't catch any exceptions that might arise from the Data layer, leaving them to be handled by the Web layer.

Example 12-13. Modified service/creature.py

```python
import os
from model.creature import Creature
if os.getenv("CRYPTID_UNIT_TEST"):
    from fake import creature as data
else:
    from data import creature as data

def get_all() -> list[Creature]:
    return data.get_all()

def get_one(name) -> Creature:
    return data.get_one(name)

def create(creature: Creature) -> Creature:
    return data.create(creature)

def modify(name: str, creature: Creature) -> Creature:
    return data.modify(name, creature)

def delete(name: str) -> None:
    return data.delete(name)
```

Example 12-14 has the corresponding unit tests.

Example 12-14. Service tests in test/unit/service/test_creature.py

```python
import os
os.environ["CRYPTID_UNIT_TEST"]= "true"
import pytest

from model.creature import Creature
from error import Missing, Duplicate
from data import creature as data

@pytest.fixture
def sample() -> Creature:
    return Creature(name="yeti",
        aka:"Abominable Snowman",
        country="CN",
        area="Himalayas",
        description="Handsome Himalayan")

def test_create(sample):
    resp = data.create(sample)
    assert resp == sample

def test_create_duplicate(sample):
    resp = data.create(sample)
    assert resp == sample
```

```
    with pytest.raises(Duplicate):
        resp = data.create(sample)

def test_get_exists(sample):
    resp = data.create(sample)
    assert resp == sample
    resp = data.get_one(sample.name)
    assert resp == sample

def test_get_missing():
    with pytest.raises(Missing):
        _ = data.get_one("boxturtle")

def test_modify(sample):
    sample.country = "CA" # Canada!
    resp = data.modify(sample.name, sample)
    assert resp == sample

def test_modify_missing():
    bob: Creature = Creature(name="bob", country="US", area="*",
        description="some guy", aka="??")
    with pytest.raises(Missing):
        _ = data.modify(bob.name, bob)
```

Data

The Data layer is simpler to test in isolation, because there's no worry about acciden-
tally calling a function in an even lower layer. Unit tests should cover both the functions in this layer and the specific database queries that they use. So far, SQLite has
been the database "server" and SQL the query language. But as I mention in Chapter 14, you may decide to work with a package like SQLAlchemy, and use its SQL-
Alchemy Expression Language or its ORM. Then these would need full tests. So far,
I've kept to the lowest level: Python's DB-API and vanilla SQL queries.

Unlike the Web and Service unit tests, this time we don't need "fake" modules to
replace the existing Data layer modules. Instead, set a different environment variable
to get the Data layer to use a memory-only SQLite instance instead of a file-based
one. This doesn't require any changes to the existing Data modules, just a setting in
Example 12-15's test *before* importing any Data modules.

Example 12-15. Data unit tests test/unit/data/test_creature.py

```
import os
import pytest
from model.creature import Creature
from error import Missing, Duplicate

# set this before data import below
os.environ["CRYPTID_SQLITE_DB"] = ":memory:"
```

```
from data import creature

@pytest.fixture
def sample() -> Creature:
    return Creature(name="yeti",
        aka="Abominable Snowman",
        country="CN",
        area="Himalayas",
        description="Hapless Himalayan")

def test_create(sample):
    resp = creature.create(sample)
    assert resp == sample

def test_create_duplicate(sample):
    with pytest.raises(Duplicate):
        _ = creature.create(sample)

def test_get_one(sample):
    resp = creature.get_one(sample.name)
    assert resp == sample

def test_get_one_missing():
    with pytest.raises(Missing):
        resp = creature.get_one("boxturtle")

def test_modify(sample):
    creature.country = "JP"   # Japan!
    resp = creature.modify(sample.name, sample)
    assert resp == sample

def test_modify_missing():
    thing: Creature = Creature(name="snurfle",
        description="some thing", country="somewhere")
    with pytest.raises(Missing):
        _ = creature.modify(thing.name, thing)

def test_delete(sample):
    resp = creature.delete(sample.name)
    assert resp is None

def test_delete_missing(sample):
    with pytest.raises(Missing):
        _ = creature.delete(sample.name)
```

Automated Integration Tests

Integration tests show how well different code interacts *between* layers. But if you look for examples of this, you get many different answers. Should you test partial call trails like Web → Service, Web → Data, and so on?

To fully test every connection in an A → B → C pipeline, you'd need to test the following:

- A → B
- B → C
- A → C

And the arrows would fill a quiver if you have more than these three junctions.

Or should integration tests be essentially full tests, but with the very end piece—data storage on disk—mocked?

So far, you've been using SQLite as the database, and you can use in-memory SQLite as a double (fake) for the on-disk SQLite database. If your queries are *very* standard SQL, SQLite-in-memory may be an adequate mock for other databases as well. If not, these modules are tailored to mock specific databases:

PostgreSQL
    pgmock (*https://pgmock.readthedocs.io*)

MongoDB
    Mongomock (*https://github.com/mongomock/mongomock*)

Many
    Pytest Mock Resources (*https://pytest-mock-resources.readthedocs.io*) spins up various test databases in Docker containers, and is integrated with pytest.

Finally, you could just fire up a test database of the same kind as production. An environment variable could contain the specifics, much like the unit test/fake trick you've been using.

The Repository Pattern

Although I did not implement it for this book, the Repository pattern (*https://oreil.ly/ 3JMKH*) is an interesting approach. A *repository* is a simple intermediate in-memory data store—like the fake Data layer that you've seen here so far. This then talks to pluggable backends for real databases. It's accompanied by a *Unit of Work* pattern (*https://oreil.ly/jHGV8*), which ensures that a group of operations in a single *session* is either committed or rolled back as a whole.

So far, the database queries in this book have been atomic. For real-world database work, you may need multistep queries, and some kind of session handling. The Repository pattern also dovetails with dependency injection (*https://oreil.ly/0f0Q3*), which you've seen elsewhere in this book and probably appreciate a little by now.

Automated Full Tests

Full tests exercise all the layers together, as close to production use as possible. Most of the tests that you've already seen in this book have been full: call the Web endpoint, run through Servicetown to downtown Dataville, and return with groceries. These are closed tests. Everything is live, and you don't care how it does it, just that it does it.

You can fully test each endpoint in the overall API in two ways:

Over HTTP/HTTPS
> Write individual Python test clients that access the server. Many examples in this book have done this, with standalone clients like HTTPie, or in scripts using Requests.

Using `TestClient`
> Use this built-in FastAPI/Starlette object to access the server directly, without an overt TCP connection.

But these approaches require writing one or more tests for each endpoint. This can become medieval, and we're a few centuries past medieval now. A more recent approach is based on *property-based testing*. This takes advantage of FastAPI's auto-generated documentation. An OpenAPI *schema* called *openapi.json* is created by FastAPI every time you change a path function or path decorator in the Web layer. This schema details everything about every endpoint: arguments, return values, and so on. That's what OpenAPI is for, as described here by the OpenAPI Initiative's FAQ page (*https://www.openapis.org/faq*):

> The OAS defines a standard, programming language-agnostic interface description for REST APIs, which allows both humans and computers to discover and understand the capabilities of a service without requiring access to source code, additional documentation, or inspection of network traffic.
>
> —OAS (OpenAPI Specification)

Two packages are needed:

Hypothesis (https://hypothesis.works)
> `pip install hypothesis`

Schemathesis (https://schemathesis.readthedocs.io)
> `pip install schemathesis`

Hypothesis is the base library, and Schemathesis applies it to the OpenAPI 3.0 schema that FastAPI generates. Running Schemathesis reads this schema, generates gobs of tests with varying data (that you don't need to come up with!), and works with pytest.

To keep this brief, Example 12-16 first slims *main.py* down to its base creature and explorer endpoints.

Example 12-16. Bare-bones main.py

```
from fastapi import FastAPI
from web import explorer, creature

app = FastAPI()
app.include_router(explorer.router)
app.include_router(creature.router)
```

Example 12-17 runs the tests.

Example 12-17. Run Schemathesis tests

```
$ schemathesis http://localhost:8000/openapi.json
====================== Schemathesis test session starts ======================
Schema location: http://localhost:8000/openapi.json
Base URL: http://localhost:8000/
Specification version: Open API 3.0.2
Workers: 1
Collected API operations: 12

GET /explorer/ .                                          [  8%]
POST /explorer/ .                                         [ 16%]
PATCH /explorer/ F                                        [ 25%]
GET /explorer .                                           [ 33%]
POST /explorer .                                          [ 41%]
GET /explorer/{name} .                                    [ 50%]
DELETE /explorer/{name} .                                 [ 58%]
GET /creature/ .                                          [ 66%]
POST /creature/ .                                         [ 75%]
PATCH /creature/ F                                        [ 83%]
GET /creature/{name} .                                    [ 91%]
DELETE /creature/{name} .                                 [100%]
```

I got two F's, both in PATCH calls (modify() functions). How mortifying.

This output section is followed by one marked FAILURES, with detailed stack traces of any tests that failed. Those need to be fixed. The final section is marked SUMMARY:

```
    Performed checks:
        not_a_server_error              717 / 727 passed         FAILED

    Hint: You can visualize test results in Schemathesis.io
    by using `--report` in your CLI command.
```

That was fast, and multiple tests were not needed for each endpoint, imagining inputs that might break them. Property-based testing reads the types and constraints of the input arguments from the API schema, and generates a range of values to shoot at each endpoint.

This is yet another unexpected benefit of type hints, which at first seemed to be just nice things:

type hints → OpenAPI schema → generated documentation *and* tests

Security Testing

Security isn't one thing, but everything. You need to defend against malice but also against plain old mistakes, and even events that you have no control over. Let's defer scaling issues to the next section and deal mainly here with the analysis of potential threats.

Chapter 11 discussed authentication and authorization. These factors are always messy and error-prone. It's tempting to use clever methods to counteract clever attacks, and it's always a challenge to design protection that's easy to understand and implement.

But now that you know about Schemathesis, read its documentation (*https://oreil.ly/ v_O-Q*) on property-based testing for authentication. Just as it vastly simplified testing most of the API, it can automate much of the tests for endpoints that need authentication.

Load Testing

Load tests show how your application handles heavy traffic:

- API calls
- Database reads or writes
- Memory use
- Disk use
- Network latency and bandwidth

Some can be *full* tests that simulate an army of users clamoring to use your service; you want to be ready before that day arrives. The content in this section overlaps with that in "Performance" on page 188 and "Troubleshooting" on page 190.

Many good load testers out are there, but here I'll recommend Locust (*https:// locust.io*). With Locust, you define all your tests with plain Python scripts. It can simulate hundreds of thousands of users, all pounding away at your site, or even multiple servers, at once.

Install it locally with `pip install locust`. Your first test may be how many concurrent visitors your site can handle. This is like testing how much extreme weather a building can withstand when faced with a hurricane/earthquake/blizzard or other home insurance event. So, you need some website structural tests. Follow the Locust docs (*https://docs.locust.io*) for all the details.

But, as they say on TV, there's more! Recently, Grasshopper (*https://github.com/alteryx/locust-grasshopper*) extended Locust to do things like measuring time across multiple HTTP calls. To try this extension out, install with `pip install locust-grasshopper`.

Review

This chapter fleshed out the types of testing, with examples of pytest performing automated code testing at the unit, integration, and full levels. API tests can be automated with Schemathesis. This chapter also discussed how to expose security and performance problems before they strike.

## CHAPTER 13

Production

> If builders built buildings the way programmers wrote programs, the first woodpecker that came along would destroy civilization.
>
> —Gerald Weinberg, computer scientist

Preview

You have an application running on your local machine, and now you'd like to share it. This chapter presents many scenarios on how to move your application to production, and keep it running correctly and efficiently. Because some of the details can be *very* detailed, in some cases I'll refer to helpful external documents rather than stuffing them in here.

Deployment

All the code examples in this book so far have used a single instance of uvicorn running on localhost, port 8000. To handle lots of traffic, you want multiple servers, running on the multiple cores that modern hardware provides. You'll also need something above these servers to do the following:

- Keep them running (a *supervisor*)
- Gather and feed external requests (a *reverse proxy*)
- Return responses
- Provide HTTPS *termination* (SSL decryption)

Multiple Workers

You've probably seen another Python server called Gunicorn (*https://gunicorn.org*). This can supervise multiple workers, but it's a WSGI server, and FastAPI is based on ASGI. Luckily, there's a special Uvicorn worker class that can be managed by Gunicorn.

Example 13-1 sets up these Uvicorn workers on localhost, port 8000 (this is adapted from the official documentation (*https://oreil.ly/Svdhx*)). The quotes protect the shell from any special interpretation.

Example 13-1. Use Gunicorn with Uvicorn workers

```
$ pip install "uvicorn[standard]" gunicorn
$ gunicorn main:app --workers 4 --worker-class \
uvicorn.workers.UvicornWorker --bind 0.0.0.0:8000
```

You'll see many lines as Gunicorn does your bidding. It will start a top-level Gunicorn process, talking to four Uvicorn worker subprocesses, all sharing port 8000 on local host (0.0.0.0). Change the host, port, or number of workers if you want something else. The main:app refers to *main.py* and the FastAPI object with the variable name app. The Gunicorn docs (*https://oreil.ly/TxYIy*) claim the following:

> Gunicorn should only need 4-12 worker processes to handle hundreds or thousands of requests per second.

It turns out that Uvicorn itself can also fire up multiple Uvicorn workers, as in Example 13-2.

Example 13-2. Use Uvicorn with Uvicorn workers

```
$ uvicorn main:app --host 0.0.0.0 --port 8000 --workers 4
```

But this method doesn't do process management, so the gunicorn method is usually preferred. Other process managers exist for Uvicorn: see its official docs (*https://www.uvicorn.org/deployment*).

This handles three of the four jobs mentioned in the previous section, but not HTTPS encryption.

HTTPS

The official FastAPI HTTPS docs (*https://oreil.ly/HYRW7*), like all of the official FastAPI docs, are extremely informative. I recommend reading them, followed by Ramírez's description (*https://oreil.ly/zcUWS*) of how to add HTTPS support to FastAPI by using Traefik (*https://traefik.io*). Traefik sits "above" your web servers, similar to nginx as a reverse proxy and load balancer, but it includes that HTTPS magic.

Although the process has many steps, it's still much simpler than it used to be. In particular, you used to regularly pay big bucks to a certificate authority for a digital certificate that you could use to provide HTTPS for your site. Luckily, those authorities have been largely replaced by the free service Let's Encrypt (*https://letsencrypt.org*).

Docker

When Docker burst on the scene (in a five-minute lightning talk (*https://oreil.ly/25oef*) by Solomon Hykes of dotCloud at PyCon 2013), it was the first time most of us had ever heard of Linux containers. Over time, we learned that Docker was faster and lighter than virtual machines. Instead of emulating a full operating system, each container shared the server's Linux kernel, and isolated processes and networks into their own namespaces. Suddenly, by using the free Docker software, you could host multiple independent services on a single machine, without worrying about them stepping all over one another.

Ten years later, Docker is universally recognized and supported. If you want to host your FastAPI application on a cloud service, you'll usually need to create a *Docker image* of it first. The official FastAPI docs (*https://oreil.ly/QnwOW*) include a thorough description of how to build a Dockerized version of your FastAPI application. One step is to write a *Dockerfile*: a text file containing Docker configuration info, like what application code to use and what processes to run. Just to prove that this isn't brain surgery during a rocket launch, here's the Dockerfile from that page:

```
FROM python:3.9
WORKDIR /code
COPY ./requirements.txt /code/requirements.txt
RUN pip install --no-cache-dir --upgrade -r /code/requirements.txt
COPY ./app /code/app
CMD ["uvicorn", "app.main:app", "--host", "0.0.0.0", "--port", "80"]
```

I recommend reading the official docs, or other links that a Google search of `fastapi docker` will produce, such as "The Ultimate FastAPI Tutorial Part 13—Using Docker to Deploy Your App" (*https://oreil.ly/7TUpR*) by Christopher Samiullah.

Cloud Services

Many sources of paid or free hosting are available on the Net. Some walk-throughs on how to host FastAPI with them include the following:

- "FastAPI—Deployment" by Tutorials Point (*https://oreil.ly/DBZcm*)
- "The Ultimate FastAPI Tutorial Part 6b—Basic Deployment on Linode" by Christopher Samiullah (*https://oreil.ly/s8iar*)
- "How to Deploy a FastAPI App on Heroku for Free" by Shinichi Okada (*https://oreil.ly/A6gij*)

Kubernetes

Kubernetes grew from internal Google code for managing internal systems that were becoming ever more godawfully complex. System administrators (as they were called then) used to manually configure tools like load balancers, reverse proxies, humidors[1] and so on. Kubernetes aimed to take much of this knowledge and automate it: don't tell me *how* to handle this; tell me what you *want*. This included tasks like keeping a service running, or firing up more servers if traffic spikes.

There are many descriptions of how to deploy FastAPI on Kubernetes, including "Deploying a FastAPI Application on Kubernetes" by Sumanta Mukhopadhyay (*https://oreil.ly/ktTNu*).

Performance

FastAPI's performance is currently among the highest (*https://oreil.ly/mxabf*) of any Python web framework, even comparable to frameworks in faster languages like Go. But much of this is due to ASGI, avoiding I/O waiting with async. Python itself is a relatively slow language. The following are some tips and tricks to improve overall performance.

Async

Often a web server doesn't need to be really fast. It spends much of its time getting HTTP network requests and returning results (the Web layer in this book). In between, a web service performs business logic (the Service layer) and accesses data sources (the Data layer), and again spends much of its time on network I/O.

Whenever code in the web service has to wait for a response, it's a good candidate to use an async function (`async def` rather than `def`). This lets FastAPI and Starlette

---

1 Wait, those keep cigars fresh.

schedule the async function and do other things while waiting for it to get its response. This is one of the reasons FastAPI's benchmarks are better than WSGI-based frameworks like Flask and Django.

Performance has two aspects:

- The time to handle a single request
- The number of requests that can be handled at once

Caches

If you have a web endpoint that ultimately gets data from a static source (like a database record that changes rarely or never), it's possible to *cache* the data in a function. This could be in any of the layers. Python provides the standard functools module (*https://oreil.ly/8Kg4V*) and the functions `cache()` and `lru_cache()`.

Databases, Files, and Memory

One of the most common causes of a slow website is a missing index for a database table of sufficient size. Often you won't see the problem until your table has grown to a particular size, and then queries suddenly become much slower. In SQL, any column in a `WHERE` clause should be indexed.

In many examples in this book, the primary key of the `creature` and `explorer` tables has been the text field `name`. When the tables were created, `name` was declared the `primary key`. For the tiny tables that you've seen so far in this book, SQLite would ignore that key anyhow, since it's faster just to scan the table. But once a table gets to a decent size—say a million rows—a missing index will make a noticeable difference. The solution: run a query optimizer (*https://oreil.ly/YPR3Q*).

Even if you have a small table, you can do database load testing with Python scripts or open source tools. If you're making numerous sequential database queries, it may be possible to combine them in a single batch. If you're uploading or downloading a large file, use the streaming versions rather than a giant gulp.

Queues

If you're performing any task that takes longer than a fraction of a second (like sending a confirmation email or downsizing an image), it may be worth handing it off to a job queue like Celery (*https://docs.celeryq.dev*).

Python Itself

If your web service seems slow because it does significant computing with Python, you may want a "faster Python." Alternatives include the following:

- Use PyPy (*https://www.pypy.org*) instead of the standard CPython.
- Write a Python extension (*https://oreil.ly/BElJa*) in C, C++, or Rust.
- Convert the slow Python code to Cython (*https://cython.org*) (used by Pydantic and Uvicorn themselves).

A very intriguing recent announcement was the Mojo language (*https://oreil.ly/ C96kx*). It aims to be a complete superset of Python, with new features (using the same friendly Python syntax) that can speed up a Python example by *thousands* of times. The main author, Chris Lattner, had previously worked on compiler tools like LLVM (*https://llvm.org*), Clang (*https://clang.llvm.org*), and MLIR (*https:// mlir.llvm.org*), plus the Swift (*https://www.swift.org*) language at Apple.

Mojo aims to be a single-language solution to AI development, which now (in PyTorch and TensorFlow) requires Python/C/C++ sandwiches that are hard to develop, manage, and debug. But Mojo also would be a good general-purpose language aside from AI.

I coded in C for years and kept waiting for a successor that was as performant but as easy to use as Python. D, Go, Julia, Zig, and Rust were possibilities, but if Mojo can live up to its goals (*https://oreil.ly/EojvA*), I would use Mojo extensively.

Troubleshooting

Look bottom-up from the time and place where you encounter a problem. This includes time and space performance issues, but also logic and async traps.

Kinds of Problems

At a first glance, what HTTP response code did you get?

404
: An authentication or authorization error.

422
: Usually a Pydantic complaint about use of a model.

500
: The failure of a service behind your FastAPI one.

Logging

Uvicorn and other web servers typically write logs to stdout. You can check the log to see what call was actually made, including the HTTP verb and URL, but not data in the body, headers, or cookies.

If a particular endpoint returns a 400-level status code, you can try feeding the same input back and see if the error reoccurs. If so, my first caveman debugging instinct is to add `print()` statements in the relevant Web, Service, and Data functions.

Also, wherever you raise an exception, add details. If a database lookup fails, include the input values and specific error, like an attempt to double a unique key field.

Metrics

The terms *metrics*, *monitoring*, *observability*, and *telemetry* may seem to overlap. It's common practice in Pythonland to use the following:

- Prometheus (*https://prometheus.io*) to gather metrics
- Grafana (*https://grafana.com*) to display them
- OpenTelemetry (*https://opentelemetry.io*) to measure timing

You can apply these to all your site's layers: Web, Service, and Data. The Service ones may be more business-oriented, and the others more technical, and useful for site developers and maintainers.

Here are some links to gather FastAPI metrics:

- Prometheus FastAPI Instrumentator (*https://oreil.ly/EYJwR*)
- "Getting Started: Monitoring a FastAPI App with Grafana and Prometheus—A Step-by-Step Guide" by Zoo Codes (*https://oreil.ly/Gs90t*)
- "FastAPI Observability" page of Grafana Labs website (*https://oreil.ly/spKwe*)
- OpenTelemetry FastAPI Instrumentation (*https://oreil.ly/wDSNv*)
- "OpenTelemetry FastAPI Tutorial—Complete Implementation Guide" by Ankit Anand (*https://oreil.ly/ZpSXs*)
- OpenTelemetry Python documentation (*https://oreil.ly/nSD4G*)

Review

It's pretty clear that production is not easy. Problems include the web machinery itself, network and disk overloading, and database problems. This chapter offered hints on how to get the information you need, and where to start digging when problems pop up.

## PART IV

A Gallery

In Part III, you built a minimal website with some basic code. Now let's do something fun with it. The following chapters apply FastAPI to common web uses: forms, files, databases, charts and graphics, maps, and games.

To tie these applications together and make them more interesting than the usual dry computing book examples, we'll plunder data from an unusual source, some of which you've already glimpsed: imaginary creatures from world folklore and the explorers who pursue them. There will be yetis, but also more obscure—though no less striking—members.

## CHAPTER 14

Databases, Data Science, and a Little AI

Preview

This chapter discusses how to use FastAPI to store and retrieve data. It expands on the simple SQLite examples of Chapter 10 with the following:

- Other open source databases (relational and not)
- Higher-level uses of SQLAlchemy
- Better error checking

Data Storage Alternatives

The term *database* is unfortunately used to refer to three things:

- The server *type*, like PostgreSQL, SQLite, or MySQL
- A running instance of that *server*
- A *collection of tables* on that server

To avoid confusion—referring to an instance of the last bulleted item above as a "PostgreSQL database database database"—I'll attach other terms to indicate which one I mean.

The usual backend for a website is a database. Websites and databases are like peanut butter and jelly, and although you could conceivably store your data in other ways (or pair peanut butter with pickles), for this book we'll stick with databases.

Databases handle many problems that you would otherwise have to solve yourself with code, such as these:

- Multiple access
- Indexing
- Data consistency

The general choices for databases are as follows:

- Relational databases, with the SQL query language
- Nonrelational databases, with various query languages

Relational Databases and SQL

Python has a standard relational API definition called DB-API (*https://oreil.ly/StbE4*), and it's supported by Python driver packages for all the major databases. Table 14-1 lists some prominent relational databases and their main Python driver packages.

Table 14-1. Relational databases and Python drivers

Database	Python drivers
Open source	
SQLite (*https://www.sqlite.org*)	sqlite3 (*https://oreil.ly/TNNaA*)
PostgreSQL (*https://www.postgresql.org*)	psycopg2 (*https://oreil.ly/nLn5x*) and asyncpg (*https://oreil.ly/90pvK*)
MySQL (*https://www.mysql.com*)	MySQLdb (*https://oreil.ly/yn1fn*) and PyMySQL (*https://oreil.ly/Cmup-*)
Commercial	
Oracle (*https://www.oracle.com*)	python-oracledb (*https://oreil.ly/gynvX*)
SQL Server (*https://www.microsoft.com/en-us/sql-server*)	pyodbc (*https://oreil.ly/_UEYq*) and pymssql (*https://oreil.ly/FkKUn*)
IBM Db2 (*https://www.ibm.com/products/db2*)	ibm_db (*https://oreil.ly/3uwpD*)

The main Python packages for relational databases and SQL are as follows:

SQLAlchemy (https://www.sqlalchemy.org)
A full-featured library that can be used at many levels

SQLModel (https://sqlmodel.tiangolo.com)
A combination of SQLAlchemy and Pydantic, by the author of FastAPI

Records (https://github.com/kennethreitz/records)
From the author of the Requests package, a simple query API

SQLAlchemy

The most popular Python SQL package is SQLAlchemy. Although many explanations of SQLAlchemy discuss only its ORM, it has multiple layers, and I'll discuss these bottom-up.

Core

The base of SQLAlchemy, called *Core*, comprises the following:

- An `Engine` object that implements the DB-API standard
- URLs that express the SQL server type and driver, and the specific database collection on that server
- Client-server connection pools
- Transactions (`COMMIT` and `ROLLBACK`)
- SQL *dialect* differences among various database types
- Direct SQL (text string) queries
- Queries in the SQLAlchemy Expression Language

Some of these features, like the dialect handling, make SQLAlchemy the package of choice for working with various server types. You can use it to execute plain DB-API SQL statements or use the SQLAlchemy Expression Language.

I've been using the raw DB-API SQLite driver so far and will continue. But for larger sites or those that might need to take advantage of a special server feature, SQLAlchemy (using basic DB-API, SQLAlchemy Expression Language, or the full ORM) is well worth using.

SQLAlchemy Expression Language

The SQLAlchemy Expression Language is *not* the ORM, but another way of expressing queries against relational tables. It maps the underlying storage structures to Python classes like `Table` and `Column`, and operations to Python methods like `select()` and `insert()`. These functions translate to plain SQL strings, and you can access them to see what happened. The language is independent of SQL server types. If you find SQL difficult, this may be worth trying.

Let's compare a few examples. Example 14-1 shows the plain SQL version.

*Example 14-1. Straight SQL code for **get_one()** in* data/explorer.py

```
def get_one(name: str) -> Explorer:
    qry = "select * from explorer where name=:name"
    params = {"name": name}
```

```
    curs.execute(qry, params)
    return row_to_model(curs.fetchone())
```

Example 14-2 shows a partial SQLAlchemy Expression Language equivalent to set up the database, build the table, and perform the insertion.

Example 14-2. SQLAlchemy Expression Language for get_one()

```
from sqlalchemy import Metadata, Table, Column, Text
from sqlalchemy import connect, insert

conn = connect("sqlite:///cryptid.db")
meta = Metadata()
explorer_table = Table(
    "explorer",
    meta,
    Column("name", Text, primary_key=True),
    Column("country", Text),
    Column("description", Text),
    )
insert(explorer_table).values(
    name="Beau Buffette",
    country="US",
    description="...")
```

For more examples, some alternative documentation (*https://oreil.ly/ZGCHv*) is a bit more readable than the official pages.

ORM

An ORM expresses queries in terms of domain data models, not the relational tables and SQL logic at the base of the database machinery. The official documentation (*https://oreil.ly/x4DCi*) goes into all the details. The ORM is much more complex than the SQL expression language. Developers who prefer fully *object-oriented* patterns usually prefer ORMs.

Many books and articles on FastAPI jump right into SQLAlchemy's ORM when they come to the database section. I understand the appeal but also know that it requires you to learn another abstraction. SQLAlchemy is an excellent package, but if its abstractions don't always hold, then you have two problems. The simplest solution may be to just use SQL, and move to the Expression Language or ORM if the SQL gets too hairy.

SQLModel

The author of FastAPI combined aspects of FastAPI, Pydantic, and SQLAlchemy to make SQLModel (*https://sqlmodel.tiangolo.com*). It repurposes some development

---

techniques from the web world to relational databases. SQLModel matches SQLAl-chemy's ORM with Pydantic's data definition and validation.

SQLite

I introduced SQLite in Chapter 10, using it for the Data layer examples. It's public domain—you can't get more open sourcey than that. SQLite is used in every browser and every smartphone, making it one of the most widely deployed software packages in the world. It's often overlooked when choosing a relational database, but it's possible that multiple SQLite "servers" could support some large services as well as a beefy server like PostgreSQL.

PostgreSQL

In the early days of relational databases, IBM's System R was the pioneer, and off-shoots battled for the new market—mainly open source Ingres versus commercial Oracle. Ingres featured a query language named QUEL, and System R had SQL. Although QUEL was considered better than SQL by some, Oracle's adoption of SQL as a standard, plus IBM's influence, helped push Oracle and SQL to success.

Years later, Michael Stonebraker returned to migrate Ingres to PostgreSQL (*https:// www.postgresql.org*). Nowadays, open source developers tend to choose PostgreSQL, although MySQL was popular a few years ago and is still around.

EdgeDB

Despite the success of SQL over the years, it does have some design flaws that make queries awkward. Unlike the mathematical theory that SQL is based on (*relational calculus* by E. F. Codd), the SQL language design itself is not *composable*. Mainly, this means that it's hard to nest queries within larger ones, leading to more complex and verbose code.

So, just for fun, I'm throwing in a new relational database here. EdgeDB (*https:// www.edgedb.com*) was written (in Python!) by the author of Python's asyncio. It's described as *Post-SQL* or *graph-relational*. Under the hood, it uses PostgreSQL to handle the tough system stuff. Edge's contribution is EdgeQL (*https://oreil.ly/sdK4J*): a new query language that aims to avoid those sharp SQL edges; it's actually translated to SQL for PostgreSQL to execute. "My Experience with EdgeDB" by Ivan Daniluk (*https://oreil.ly/ciNfg*) handily compares EdgeQL and SQL. The readable illustrated official documentation (*https://oreil.ly/ce6y3*) parallels the book *Dracula*.

Could EdgeQL spread beyond EdgeDB and become an alternative to SQL? Time will tell.

Nonrelational (NoSQL) Databases

Biggies in the open source NoSQL or NewSQL world are listed in Table 14-2.

Table 14-2. NoSQL databases and Python drivers

Database	Python drivers
Redis (*https://redis.io*)	redis-py (*https://github.com/redis/redis-py*)
MongoDB (*https://www.mongodb.com*)	PyMongo (*https://pymongo.readthedocs.io*), Motor (*https://oreil.ly/Cmgtl*)
Apache Cassandra (*https://cassandra.apache.org*)	DataStax Driver for Apache Cassandra (*https://github.com/datastax/python-driver*)
Elasticsearch (*https://www.elastic.co/elasticsearch*)	Python Elasticsearch Client (*https://oreil.ly/e_bDl*)

Sometimes *NoSQL* means literally *no SQL*, but sometimes *not only SQL*. Relational databases enforce structures on data, often visualized as rectangular tables with column fields and data rows, similar to spreadsheets. To reduce redundancy and improve performance, relational databases are *normalized* with *normal forms* (rules for data and structures), such as allowing only a single value per cell (row/column intersection).

NoSQL databases relax these rules, sometimes allowing varying column/field types across individual data rows. Often the *schemas* (database designs) can be ragged structures, as you could express in JSON or Python, rather than relational boxes.

Redis

Redis is a data structure server that runs completely in memory, although it can save to and restore from disk. It closely matches Python's own data structures and has become extremely popular.

MongoDB

MongoDB is sort of the PostgreSQL of NoSQL servers. A *collection* is the equivalent of a SQL table, and a *document* is the equivalent of a SQL table row. Another difference, and the main reason for a NoSQL database in the first place, is that you don't need to define what a document looks like. In other words, there's no fixed *schema*. A document is like a Python dictionary, with any string as a key.

Cassandra

Cassandra is a large-scale database that can be distributed across hundreds of nodes. It's written in Java.

An alternative database called ScyllaDB (*https://www.scylladb.com*) is written in C++ and claims to be compatible with Cassandra but more performant.

Elasticsearch

Elasticsearch (*https://www.elastic.co/elasticsearch*) is more like a database index than a database itself. It's often used for full-text search.

NoSQL Features in SQL Databases

As noted previously, relational databases were traditionally normalized—constrained to follow different levels of rules called *normal forms*. One basic rule was that the value in each cell (row-column intersection) had to be a *scalar* (no arrays or other structures).

NoSQL (or *document*) databases supported JSON directly and were usually your only choice if you had "uneven" or "ragged" data structures. They were often *denormalized*: all the data needed for a document was included with that document. In SQL, you often needed to *join* across tables to build a full document.

However, recent revisions of the SQL standard have allowed JSON data to be stored in relational databases also. Some relational databases now let you store complex (nonscalar) data in table cells, and even search and index within them. JSON functions are supported in various ways for SQLite (*https://oreil.ly/h_FNn*), PostgreSQL (*https://oreil.ly/awYrc*), MySQL (*https://oreil.ly/OA_sT*), Oracle (*https://oreil.ly/osOYk*), and others.

SQL with JSON can be the best of both worlds. SQL databases have been around much longer and have really useful features such as foreign keys and secondary indexes. Also, SQL is fairly standardized up to a point, and NoSQL query languages are all different.

Finally, new data design and query languages are trying to combine SQL and NoSQL advantages, like EdgeQL that I mentioned earlier.

So, if you can't fit your data into the rectangular relational box, look at a NoSQL database, a relational database with JSON support, or a "Post-SQL" database.

Database Load Testing

This book is mainly about FastAPI, but websites are so frequently tied to databases.

The data examples in this book have been tiny. To really stress-test a database, millions of items would be great. Rather than think of things to add, it's easier use a Python package like Faker (*https://faker.readthedocs.io*). Faker can generate many kinds of data quickly—names, places, or special types that you define.

In Example 14-3, Faker pumps out names and countries, which are then loaded by load() into SQLite.

Example 14-3. Load fake explorers in test_load.py

```
from faker import Faker
from time import perf_counter

def load():
    from error import Duplicate
    from data.explorer import create
    from model.explorer import Explorer

    f = Faker()
    NUM = 100_000
    t1 = perf_counter()
    for row in range(NUM):
        try:
            create(Explorer(name=f.name(),
                country=f.country(),
                description=f.description))
        except Duplicate:
            pass
    t2 = perf_counter()
    print(NUM, "rows")
    print("write time:", t2-t1)

def read_db():
    from data.explorer import get_all

    t1 = perf_counter()
    _ = get_all()
    t2 = perf_counter()
    print("db read time:", t2-t1)

def read_api():
    from fastapi.testclient import TestClient
    from main import app

    t1 = perf_counter()
    client = TestClient(app)
    _ = client.get("/explorer/")
    t2 = perf_counter()
    print("api read time:", t2-t1)

load()
read_db()
read_db()
read_api()
```

You're catching the Duplicate exception in load() and ignoring it, because Faker generates names from a limited list and is likely to repeat one now and then. So the result may be less than 100,000 explorers loaded.

Also, you're calling `read_db()` twice, to remove any startup time as SQLite does the query. Then `read_api()` timing should be fair. Example 14-4 fires it up.

Example 14-4. Test database query performance

```
$ python test_load.py
100000 rows
write time: 14.868232927983627
db read time: 0.4025074450764805
db read time: 0.39750714192632586
api read time: 2.597553930943832
```

The API read time for all explorers was much slower than the Data layer's read time. Some of this is probably overhead from FastAPI's conversion of the response to JSON. Also, the initial write time to the database wasn't very zippy. It wrote one explorer at a time, because the Data layer API has a single `create()` function, but not a `create_many()`; on the read side, the API can return one (`get_one()`) or all (`get_all()`). So, if you ever want to do bulk loading, it might be good to add a new Data load function and a new Web endpoint (with restricted authorization).

Also, if you expect any table in your database to grow to 100,000 rows, maybe you shouldn't allow random users to get all of them in one API call. Pagination would be useful, or a way to download a single CSV file from the table.

Data Science and AI

Python has become the most prominent language in data science in general, and machine learning in particular. So much data massaging is needed, and Python is good at that.

Sometimes developers have used external tools (*https://oreil.ly/WFHo9*) like pandas to do the data manipulation that's too tricky in SQL.

PyTorch (*https://pytorch.org*) is one of the most popular ML tools, because it leverages Python's strengths in data manipulation. The underlying computations may be in C or C++ for speed, but Python or Go are well-suited for the "higher" data-integration tasks. (The Mojo (*https://www.modular.com/mojo*) language, a superset of Python, may handle both the high and low ends if it succeeds as planned. Although a general-purpose language, it specifically addresses some of the current complexity in AI development.)

A new Python tool called Chroma (*https://www.trychroma.com*) is a database, similar to SQLite, but tailored to machine learning, specifically large language models (LLMs). Read the Getting Started page (*https://oreil.ly/W59nn*) to, you know, get started.

Although AI development is complex and moving fast, you can try out some AI with Python on your own machine without spending the megabucks that were behind GPT-4 and ChatGPT. Let's build a small FastAPI web interface to a small AI model.

 Model has different meanings in AI and Pydantic/FastAPI. In Pydantic, a model is a Python class that bundles related data fields. AI models cover a broad range of techniques for determining patterns in data.

Hugging Face (*https://huggingface.co*) provides free AI models, datasets, and Python code to use them. First, install PyTorch and Hugging Face code:

```
$ pip install torch torchvision
$ pip install transformers
```

Example 14-5 shows a FastAPI application that uses Hugging Face's transformers module to access a pretrained mid-sized open source machine language model and try to answer your prompts. (This was adapted from a command-line example on the YouTube channel CodeToTheMoon.)

Example 14-5. Top-level LLM test (ai.py)

```
from fastapi import FastAPI

app = FastAPI()

from transformers import (AutoTokenizer,
    AutoModelForSeq2SeqLM, GenerationConfig)
model_name = "google/flan-t5-base"
tokenizer = AutoTokenizer.from_pretrained(model_name)
model = AutoModelForSeq2SeqLM.from_pretrained(model_name)
config = GenerationConfig(max_new_tokens=200)

@app.get("/ai")
def prompt(line: str) -> str:
    tokens = tokenizer(line, return_tensors="pt")
    outputs = model.generate(**tokens,
        generator_config=config)
    result = tokenizer.batch_decode(outputs,
        skip_special_tokens=True)
    return result[0]
```

Run this with `uvicorn ai:app` (as always, first make sure you don't have another web server still running on `localhost`, port 8000). Feed the */ai* endpoint questions and get answers, like this (note the double == for an HTTPie query parameter):

```
$ http -b localhost:8000/ai line=="What are you?"
"a sailor"
```

This is a fairly small model, and as you can see, it doesn't answer questions especially well. I tried other prompts (`line` arguments) and got equally noteworthy answers:

- Q: Are cats better than dogs?
- A: No
- Q: What does bigfoot eat for breakfast?
- A: A squid
- Q: Who comes down the chimney?
- A: A squealing pig
- Q: What group was John Cleese in?
- A: The Beatles
- Q: What has nasty pointy teeth?
- A: A teddy bear

These questions may get different answers at different times! Once the same endpoint said that Bigfoot eats sand for breakfast. In AI-speak, answers like this are called *hallucinations*. You can get better answers by using a larger model, like `google/flan-75-xl`, but it will take longer to download model data and respond on a personal computer. And of course, models like ChatGPT were trained on all the data they could find (using every CPU, GPU, TPU, and any other kind of PU), and will give excellent answers.

Review

This chapter expanded on the use of SQLite we went over in Chapter 10 to other SQL databases, and even NoSQL ones. It also showed how some SQL databases can do NoSQL tricks with JSON support. Finally, it talked about the uses of database and special data tools that have become more important as machine learning continues its explosive growth.

## CHAPTER 15

Files

Preview

Besides fielding API requests and traditional content like HTML, web servers are expected to handle file transfers in both directions. Very large files may need to be transferred in *chunks* that don't use too much of the system's memory. You can also provide access to a directory of files (and subdirectories, to any depth) with `Static Files`.

Multipart Support

To handle large files, FastAPI's uploading and downloading features need these extra modules:

Python-Multipart (https://oreil.ly/FUBk7)
```
pip install python-multipart
```

aio-files (https://oreil.ly/OZYYR)
```
pip install aiofiles
```

Uploading Files

FastAPI targets API development, and most of the examples in this book have used JSON requests and responses. But in the next chapter you'll see forms, which are handled differently. This chapter covers files, which are treated like forms in some ways.

FastAPI offers two techniques for file uploads: `File()` and `UploadFile`.

File()

File() is used as the type for a direct file upload. Your path function may be synchronous (def) or asynchronous (async def), but the asynchronous version is better because it won't tie up your web server while the file is uploading.

FastAPI will pull up the file in chunks and reassemble it in memory, so File() should be used for only relatively small files. Instead of assuming that the input is JSON, FastAPI encodes a file as a form element.

Let's write the code to request a file and test it. You can grab any file on your machine to test with, or download one from a site like Fastest Fish (*https://oreil.ly/EnlH-*). I grabbed a 1 KB file from there and saved it locally as *1KB.bin*.

In Example 15-1, add these lines to your top *main.py*.

Example 15-1. Handle a small file upload with FastAPI

```
from fastapi import File

@app.post("/small")
async def upload_small_file(small_file: bytes = File()) -> str:
    return f"file size: {len(small_file)}"
```

After Uvicorn restarts, try an HTTPie test in Example 15-2.

Example 15-2. Upload a small file with HTTPie

```
$ http -f -b POST http://localhost:8000/small small_file@1KB.bin
"file size: 1000"
```

Here are a few notes on this test:

- You need to include -f (or --form), because files are uploaded like forms, not as JSON text.
- small_file@1KB.bin:

  small_file
  : Matches the variable name small_file in the FastAPI path function in Example 15-1

  @
  : HTTPie's shorthand to make a form

  1KB.bin
  : The file that is being uploaded

Example 15-3 is an equivalent programmatic test.

Example 15-3. Upload a small file with Requests

```
$ python
>>> import requests
>>> url = "http://localhost:8000/small"
>>> files = {'small_file': open('1KB.bin', 'rb')}
>>> resp = requests.post(url, files=files)
>>> print(resp.json())
file size: 1000
```

UploadFile

For large files, it's better to use `UploadFile`. This creates a Python `SpooledTemporary File` object, mostly on the server's disk instead of in memory. This is a Python *file-like* object, which supports the methods `read()`, `write()`, and `seek()`. Example 15-4 shows this, and also uses `async def` instead of `def` to avoid blocking the web server while file pieces are uploading.

Example 15-4. Upload a big file with FastAPI (add to main.py*)*

```
from fastapi import UploadFile

@app.post("/big")
async def upload_big_file(big_file: UploadFile) -> str:
    return f"file size: {big_file.size}, name: {big_file.filename}"
```

 `File()` created a bytes object and needed the parentheses. `Upload File` is a different class of object.

If Uvicorn's starter motor isn't worn out yet, it's test time. This time, Examples 15-5 through 15-6 use a 1 GB file (*1GB.bin*) that I grabbed from Fastest Fish.

Example 15-5. Test a big file upload with HTTPie

```
$ http -f -b POST http://localhost:8000/big big_file@1GB.bin
"file size: 1000000000, name: 1GB.bin"
```

Example 15-6. Test a big file upload with Requests

```
>>> import requests
>>> url = "http://localhost:8000/big"
>>> files = {'big_file': open('1GB.bin', 'rb')}
>>> resp = requests.post(url, files=files)
>>> print(resp.json())
file size: 1000000000, name: 1GB.bin
```

Downloading Files

Sadly, gravity doesn't make files download faster. Instead, we'll use equivalents of the upload methods.

FileResponse

First, in Example 15-7, is the all-at-once version, `FileResponse`.

Example 15-7. Download a small file with `FileResponse` (add to main.py*)*

```
from fastapi.responses import FileResponse

@app.get("/small/{name}")
async def download_small_file(name):
    return FileResponse(name)
```

There's a test around here somewhere. First, put the file *1KB.bin* in the same directory as *main.py*. Now, run Example 15-8.

Example 15-8. Download a small file with HTTPie

```
$ http -b http://localhost:8000/small/1KB.bin

-----------------------------------------
| NOTE: binary data not shown in terminal |
-----------------------------------------
```

If you don't trust that suppression message, Example 15-9 pipes the output to a utility like wc to ensure that you got 1,000 bytes back.

Example 15-9. Download a small file with HTTPie, with byte count

```
$ http -b http://localhost:8000/small/1KB.bin | wc -c
    1000
```

StreamingResponse

Similar to `FileUpload`, it's better to download large files with `StreamingResponse`, which returns the file in chunks. Example 15-10 shows this, with an `async def` path function to avoid blocking when the CPU isn't being used. I'm skipping error checking for now; if the file `path` doesn't exist, the `open()` call will raise an exception.

Example 15-10. Return a big file with StreamingResponse (add to main.py*)*

```
from pathlib import path
from typing import Generator
from fastapi.responses import StreamingResponse

def gen_file(path: str) -> Generator:
    with open(file=path, mode="rb") as file:
        yield file.read()

@app.get("/download_big/{name}")
async def download_big_file(name:str):
    gen_expr = gen_file(file_path=path)
    response = StreamingResponse(
        content=gen_expr,
        status_code=200,
    )
    return response
```

`gen_expr` is the *generator expression* returned by the *generator function* `gen_file()`. `StreamingResponse` uses it for its iterable `content` argument, so it can download the file in chunks.

Example 15-11 is the accompanying test. (This first needs the file *1GB.bin* alongside *main.py*, and will take a *little* longer.)

Example 15-11. Download a big file with HTTPie

```
$ http -b http://localhost:8000/big/1GB.bin | wc -c
 1000000000
```

Serving Static Files

Traditional web servers can treat server files as though they were on a normal filesystem. FastAPI lets you do this with `StaticFiles`.

For this example, let's make a directory of (boring) free files for users to download:

- Make a directory called *static*, at the same level as *main.py*. (This can have any name; I'm calling it *static* only to help remember why I made it.)
- Put a text file called *abc.txt* in it, with the text contents abc :).

Example 15-12 will serve any URL that starts with */static* (you could also have used any text string here) with files from the *static* directory.

Example 15-12. Serve everything in a directory with StaticFiles *(add to* main.py*)*

```
from pathlib import Path
from fastapi import FastAPI
from fastapi.staticfiles import StaticFiles

# Directory containing main.py:
top = Path(__file__).resolve.parent

app.mount("/static",
    StaticFiles(directory=f"{top}/static", html=True),
    name="free")
```

That top calculation ensures that you put static alongside *main.py*. The __file__ variable is the full pathname of this file (*main.py*).

Example 15-13 is one way to manually test Example 15-12.

Example 15-13. Get a static file

```
$ http -b localhost:8000/static/abc.txt
abc :)
```

What about that html=True argument that you passed to StaticFiles()? That makes it work a little more like a traditional server, returning an *index.html* file if one exists in that directory, but you didn't ask for *index.html* explicitly in the URL. So, let's create an *index.html* file in the *static* directory with the contents Oh. Hi!, and then test with Example 15-14.

Example 15-14. Get an index.html *file from* /static

```
$ http -b localhost:8000/static/
Oh. Hi!
```

You can have as many files (and subdirectories with files, etc.) as you want. Make a subdirectory *xyz* under *static* and put two files there:

xyx.txt
> Contains the text xyz :(.

index.html
> Contains the text How did you find me?

I won't include the examples here. Try them yourself, with I hope more naming imagination.

Review

This chapter showed how to upload and download files—small, large, even giganti-ferous. Plus, you learned how to serve *static files* in nostalgic (non-API) web style from a directory.

## CHAPTER 16

Forms and Templates

Preview

Although the *API* in *FastAPI* is a hint of its main focus, FastAPI can also handle traditional web content. This chapter talks about standard HTML forms and templates for inserting data into HTML.

Forms

As you've seen, FastAPI was mainly designed to build APIs, and its default input is JSON. But that doesn't mean that it can't serve standard banana HTML, forms, and friends.

FastAPI supports data from HTML forms much as it does from other sources like `Query` and `Path`, using the `Form` dependency.

You'll need the package Python-Multipart for any FastAPI forms work, so run `pip install python-multipart` if you need to. Also, the *static* directory from Chapter 15 will be needed to house the test forms in this chapter.

Let's redo Example 3-11, but provide the `who` value via a form instead of a JSON string. (Call this path function `greet2()` to avoid clobbering the old `greet()` path function if it's still around.) Add Example 16-1 to *main.py*.

Example 16-1. Get a value from a GET form

```
from fastapi import FastAPI, Form

app = FastAPI()

@app.get("/who2")
```

```
def greet2(name: str = Form()):
    return f"Hello, {name}?"
```

The main difference is that the value comes from Form instead of Path, Query, and the others from Chapter 3.

Try an initial form test with HTTPie in Example 16-2 (you need that -f to upload with form encoding rather than as JSON).

Example 16-2. Form GET request with HTTPie

```
$ http -f -b GET localhost:8000/who2 name="Bob Frapples"
"Hello, Bob Frapples?"
```

You could also send a request from a standard HTML form file. Chapter 15 showed how to make a directory called *static* (accessed under the URL */static*) that could house anything, including HTML files, so in Example 16-3, let's put this file (*form1.html*) there.

Example 16-3. Form GET request (static/form1.html)

```
<form action="http://localhost:8000/who2" method="get">
Say hello to my little friend:
<input type="text" name="name" value="Bob Frapples">
<input type="submit">
</form>
```

If you ask your browser to load *http://localhost:8000/static/form1.html*, you'll see a form. If you fill in any test string, you'll get this back:

```
"detail":[{"loc":["body","name"],
           "msg":"field required",
           "type":"value_error.missing"}]}
```

Huh?

Look at the window where Uvicorn is running to see what its log says:

```
INFO:      127.0.0.1:63502 -
  "GET /who2?name=rr23r23 HTTP/1.1"
  422 Unprocessable Entity
```

Why did this form send name as a query parameter when we had it in a form field? That turns out to be an HTML weirdness, documented on the W3C website (*https://oreil.ly/e6CJb*). Also, if you had any query parameters in your URL, it will erase them and replace them with name.

So, why did HTTPie handle it as expected? I don't know. It's an inconsistency to be aware of.

The official HTML incantation is to change the action from a GET to a POST. So let's add a POST endpoint for */who2* to *main.py* in Example 16-4.

Example 16-4. Get a value from a POST form

```
from fastapi import FastAPI, Form

app = FastAPI()

@app.post("/who2")
def greet3(name: str = Form()):
    return f"Hello, {name}?"
```

Example 16-5 is *stuff/form2.html*, with get changed to post.

Example 16-5. Form POST request (static/form2.html)

```
<form action="http://localhost:8000/who2" method="post">
Say hello to my little friend:
<input type="text" name="name">
<input type="submit">
</form>
```

Ask your browser to get off its digital haunches and get this new form for you. Fill in **Bob Frapples** and submit the form. This time, you'll get the result that you got from HTTPie:

```
"Hello, Bob Frapples?"
```

So, if you're submitting forms from HTML files, use POST.

Templates

You may have seen the word game *Mad Libs*. You ask people to provide a sequence of words—nouns, verbs, or something more specific—and you enter them into labeled places in a page of text. Once you have all the words, you read the text with the inserted values, and hilarity ensues, sometimes with embarrassment.

Well, a web *template* is similar, though usually without the embarrassment. A template contains a bunch of text with slots for data to be inserted by the server. Its usual purpose is to generate HTML with variable content, unlike the *static* HTML of Chapter 15.

Users of Flask are very familiar with its companion project, the template engine Jinja (*https://jinja.palletsprojects.com*) (also often called *Jinja2*). FastAPI supports Jinja, as well as other template engines.

Make a directory called *template* alongside *main.py* to house Jinja-enhanced HTML files. Inside, make a file called *list.html*, as in Example 16-6.

Example 16-6. Define a template file (template/list.html)

```html
<html>
<table bgcolor="#eeeeee">
  <tr>
    <th colspan=3>Creatures</th>
  </tr>
  <tr>
    <th>Name</th>
    <th>Description</th>
    <th>Country</th>
    <th>Area</th>
    <th>AKA</th>
  </tr>
{% for creature in creatures: %}
  <tr>
    <td>{{ creature.name }}</td>
    <td>{{ creature.description }}</td>
    <td>{{ creature.country }}</td>
    <td>{{ creature.area }}</td>
    <td>{{ creature.aka }}</td>
  </tr>
{% endfor %}
</table>

<br>

<table bgcolor="#dddddd">
  <tr>
    <th colspan=2>Explorers</th>
  </tr>
  <tr>
    <th>Name</th>
    <th>Country</th>
    <th>Description</th>
  </tr>
{% for explorer in explorers: %}
  <tr>
    <td>{{ explorer.name }}</td>
    <td>{{ explorer.country }}</td>
    <td>{{ explorer.description }}</td>
  </tr>
{% endfor %}
</table>
</html>
```

I don't care how it looks, so there's no CSS, just the ancient pre-CSS `bgcolor` table attribute to distinguish the two tables.

Double curly braces enclose Python variables that should be inserted, and {% and %} enclose `if` statements, `for` loops, and other controls. See the Jinja documentation (*https://jinja.palletsprojects.com*) for the syntax and examples.

This template expects to be passed Python variables called `creatures` and `explorers`, which are lists of `Creature` and `Explorer` objects.

Example 16-7 shows what to add to *main.py* to set up templates and use the one from Example 16-6. It feeds `creatures` and `explorers` to the template, using modules under the *fake* directory from previous chapters, which provided test data if the database was empty or not connected.

Example 16-7. Configure templates and use one (main.py)

```
from pathlib import Path
from fastapi import FastAPI, Request
from fastapi.templating import Jinja2Templates

app = FastAPI()

top = Path(__file__).resolve().parent

template_obj = Jinja2Templates(directory=f"{top}/template")

# Get some small predefined lists of our buddies:
from fake.creature import fakes as fake_creatures
from fake.explorer import fakes as fake_explorers

@app.get("/list")
def explorer_list(request: Request):
    return template_obj.TemplateResponse("list.html",
        {"request": request,
        "explorers": fake_explorers,
        "creatures": fake_creatures})
```

Ask your favorite browser, or even one that you don't like very well, for *http://localhost:8000/list*, and you should get Figure 16-1 back.

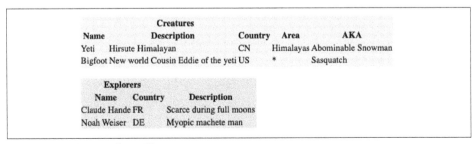

Figure 16-1. Output from /list

Review

This chapter was a quick overview of how FastAPI handles non-API topics like forms and templates. Along with the previous chapter on files, these are traditional bread-and-butter web tasks that you'll encounter often.

## CHAPTER 17

Data Discovery and Visualization

Preview

Although FastAPI does have *API* in its name, it can serve more things than APIs. This chapter shows you how to generate tables, plots, graphs, and maps from data, using a small database of imaginary creatures from around the world.

Python and Data

Python has become very popular in the last few years for many reasons:

- Ease of learning
- Clean syntax
- Rich standard library
- Huge number of high-quality third-party packages
- Special emphasis on data manipulation, conversion, and introspection

The last point has always been relevant for traditional ETL tasks for database creation. A nonprofit group called PyData (*https://pydata.org*) even organizes conferences and develops tools for open source data analysis with Python. The popularity of Python also reflects the recent surge in AI and the need for tools to prepare the data that feeds AI models.

In this chapter, we'll try some Python data packages and see how they relate to modern Python web development and FastAPI.

PSV Text Output

In this section, we'll use the creatures listed in Appendix B. The data is in this book's GitHub repo, in the pipe-separated file *cryptid.psv* and the SQLite database *cryptid.db*. Comma-separated (*.csv*) and tab-separated (*.tsv*) files are common, but commas are used within the data cells themselves, and tabs are sometimes hard to distinguish from other whitespace. The pipe character (|) is distinct, and rare enough in standard text to serve as a good separator.

Let's try the *.psv* text file first, using just text output examples for simplicity, and then go on to full web examples using the SQLite database.

The initial header line of the *.psv* file contains the names of the fields:

- `name`
- `country` (* means many countries)
- `area` (optional, US state or other country area)
- `description`
- `aka` (also known as)

The rest of the lines in the file describe one creature at a time, with the fields in that order, separated by a | character.

CSV

Example 17-1 reads the creature data into Python data structures. First, the pipe-separated file *cryptids.psv* can be read with the standard Python csv package, yielding a list of tuples, where each tuple represents a line of data from the file. (The csv package also includes a `DictReader` that returns a list of dicts instead.) The first line of this file is a header with the names of the columns; without this, we could still supply the headers through arguments to csv functions.

I'm including type hints in the examples, but you can drop these if you have an older version of Python, and the code will still work. Let's print only the header and first five lines, to save a few trees.[1]

---

1 If there are any trees like Tolkien's Ents, we don't want them lumbering up to our doors some night to have a word.

Example 17-1. Read PSV file with csv (load_csv.py)

```
import csv
import sys

def read_csv(fname: str) -> list[tuple]:
    with open(fname) as file:
        data = [row for row in csv.reader(file, delimiter="|")]
    return data

if __name__ == "__main__":
    data = read_csv(sys.argv[1])
    for row in data[0:5]:
        print(row)
```

Now run the test in Example 17-2.

Example 17-2. Test CSV database loading

```
$ python load_csv.py cryptid.psv
['name', 'country', 'area', 'description', 'aka']
['Abaia', 'FJ', ' ', 'Lake eel', ' ']
['Afanc', 'UK', 'CYM', 'Welsh lake monster', ' ']
['Agropelter', 'US', 'ME', 'Forest twig flinger', ' ']
['Akkorokamui', 'JP', ' ', 'Giant Ainu octopus', ' ']
['Albatwitch', 'US', 'PA', 'Apple stealing mini Bigfoot', ' ']
```

python-tabulate

Let's try one more open source tool, python-tabulate (*https://oreil.ly/L0f6k*), that is specifically designed for tabular output. You'll need to run `pip install tabulate` first. Example 17-3 shows the code.

Example 17-3. Read PSV file with python-tabulate (load_tabulate.py)

```
from tabulate import tabulate
import sys

def read_csv(fname: str) -> list[tuple]:
    with open(fname) as file:
        data = [row for row in csv.reader(file, delimiter="|")]
    return data

if __name__ == "__main__":
    data = read_csv(sys.argv[1])
    print(tabulate(data[0:5]))
```

Run Example 17-3 in Example 17-4.

Example 17-4. Run the tabulate load script

```
$ python load_tabulate.py cryptid.psv
-----------  -------  ----  ------------------  ---
Name         Country  Area  Description         AKA
Abaia        FJ             Lake eel
Afanc        UK       CYM   Welsh lake monster
Agropelter   US       ME    Forest twig flinger
Akkorokamui  JP             Giant Ainu octopus
-----------  -------  ----  ------------------  ---
```

pandas

The two previous examples were mostly output formatters. Pandas (*https:// pandas.pydata.org*) is an excellent tool for slicing and dicing data. It goes beyond the standard Python data structures with advanced constructs like the DataFrame (*https://oreil.ly/j-8eh*): a combination of a table, dictionary, and series. It can also read *.csv* and other character-separated files. Example 17-5 is like the previous examples, but pandas returns a DataFrame instead of a list of tuples.

Example 17-5. Read PSV file with pandas (load_pandas.py)

```
import pandas
import sys

def read_pandas(fname: str) -> pandas.DataFrame:
    data = pandas.read_csv(fname, sep="|")
    return data

if __name__ == "__main__":
    data = read_pandas(sys.argv[1])
    print(data.head(5))
```

Run Example 17-5 in Example 17-6.

Example 17-6. Run the pandas load script

```
$ python load_pandas.py cryptid.psv
          name country area                 description aka
0        Abaia      FJ                          Lake eel
1        Afanc      UK  CYM          Welsh lake monster
2   Agropelter      US  ME          Forest twig flinger
3  Akkorokamui      JP                 Giant Ainu octopus
4   Albatwitch      US  PA  Apple stealing mini Bigfoot
```

Pandas has a metric boatload of interesting functions, so take a look.

SQLite Data Source and Web Output

For the rest of the examples in this chapter, you'll read creature data from the SQLite database, using some of the website code from earlier chapters. Then you'll slice, dice, and marinate the data with different recipes. Instead of simple text output, you'll install each example into our ever-growing cryptid website. You'll need a few additions to our existing Web, Service, and Data levels.

First, you need a Web-level function and an associated HTTP GET route to return all the creature data. And you already have one! Let's make a web call to get everything, but again show only the first few lines (trees, you know). That's Example 17-7, right here.

Example 17-7. Run the creature download test (truncated; trees are watching)

```
$ http -b localhost:8000/creature
[
    {
        "aka": "AKA",
        "area": "Area",
        "country": "Country",
        "description": "Description",
        "name": "Name"
    },
    {
        "aka": " ",
        "area": " ",
        "country": "FJ",
        "description": "Lake eel",
        "name": "Abaia"
    },
...
]
```

Chart/Graph Packages

Now we can go beyond text to GUIs. Some of the most useful and popular Python packages for graphical data displays include the following:

Matplotlib (https://matplotlib.org)
    Extensive, but needs some fiddling to get the prettiest results

Plotly (https://plotly.com/python)
    Similar to Matplotlib and Seaborn, with an emphasis on interactive graphs

Dash (https://dash.plotly.com)
    Built on Plotly as a sort of data dashboard

Seaborn (https://seaborn.pydata.org)
Built on Matplotlib and offers a higher-level interface, but with less graph types

Bokeh (http://bokeh.org)
Integrates with JavaScript to provide dashboard views of very large datasets

How can you decide? You can consider the following criteria:

- Graph types (e.g., scatter, bar, line)
- Styling
- Ease of use
- Performance
- Data limits

Comparisons like "Top 6 Python Libraries for Visualization: Which One to Use?" (*https://oreil.ly/10Nsw*) by khuyentran1476 can help you choose. In the end, the choice often comes down to the one that you figure out enough about first. For this chapter, I chose Plotly, which can create attractive plots without too much coding.

Chart Example 1: Test

Plotly is an open source (free) Python library with multiple levels of control and detail:

Plotly Express (https://plotly.com/python/plotly-express)
A minimal Plotly library

Plotly (https://plotly.com/python)
The main library

Dash (https://dash.plotly.com)
Data application tools

There is also Dash Enterprise (*https://dash.plotly.com/dash-enterprise*), which, like almost anything with *Enterprise* in its name (including spaceship models) costs money.

What can we actually show from the creature data? Charts and graphs have some common forms:

- Scatter
- Line
- Bar
- Histogram
- Box (statistical)

Our data fields are all strings, intentionally minimal to keep the examples from overwhelming the logic and integration steps. For each example, we'll read all the creature data from the SQLite database using code from previous chapters, and adding Web and Service functions to select particular data to feed to the plot library functions.

First, install Plotly, and a library needed by Plotly to export images:

- `pip install plotly`
- `pip install kaleido`

Then, in Example 17-8, add a test function to *web/creature.py* to see if we have the right pieces, in the right places.

Example 17-8. Add a test plot endpoint (edit web/creature.py*)*

```
# (insert these lines in web/creature.py)

from fastapi import Response
import plotly.express as px

@router.get("/test")
def test():
    df = px.data.iris()
    fig = px.scatter(df, x="sepal_width", y="sepal_length", color="species")
    fig_bytes = fig.to_image(format="png")
    return Response(content=fig_bytes, media_type="image/png")
```

The documentation routinely recommends calling `fig.show()` to show the image that you just created, but we're trying to fit in with how FastAPI and Starlette do things.

So first you get `fig_bytes` (the actual `bytes` content of the image); then you return a custom `Response` object.

After you've added this endpoint to *web/creature.py* and restarted the web server (automatically if you ran Uvicorn with `--reload`), try accessing this new endpoint by typing **localhost:8000/creature/test** into your browser's location bar. You should see Figure 17-1.

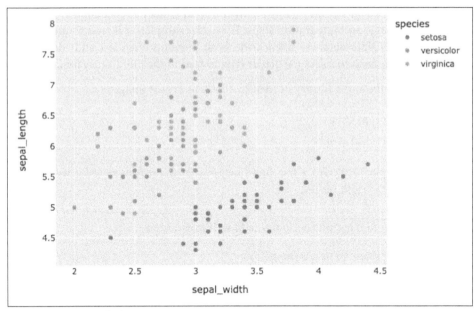

Figure 17-1. Test Plotly image

If you got a weird error from Uvicorn like `ValueError: 'not' is not a valid parameter name`, then update Pydantic to fix a bug: `pip install -U pydantic`.

Chart Example 2: Histogram

If all is well, let's start playing with our creature data. We'll add a `plot()` function to *web/creature.py*. We'll get all the creature data from the database via the `get_all()` functions in *service/creature.py* and *data/creature.py*. Then we'll extract what we want and use Plotly to display various images of the results.

For our first trick (Example 17-9), we'll just use the `name` field and make a bar chart indicating the number of creatures' names that start with each letter.

Example 17-9. Bar chart of creature name initials

```
# (insert these lines in web/creature.py)

from collections import Counter
from fastapi import Response
import plotly.express as px
from service.creature import get_all

@router.get("/plot")
def plot():
    creatures = get_all()
```

```
letters = "ABCDEFGHIJKLMNOPQRSTUVWXYZ"
counts = Counter(creature.name[0] for creature in creatures)
y = { letter: counts.get(letter, 0) for letter in letters }
fig = px.histogram(x=list(letters), y=y, title="Creature Names",
    labels={"x": "Initial", "y": "Initial"})
fig_bytes = fig.to_image(format="png")
return Response(content=fig_bytes, media_type="image/png")
```

Type **localhost:8000/creature/plot** into your browser's location bar. You should see Figure 17-2.

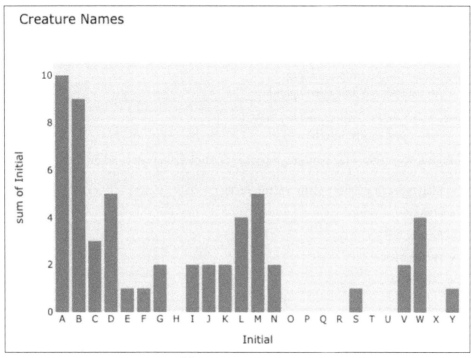

Figure 17-2. Creature name initial histogram

Map Packages

If you try to Google **Python** and **maps**, you'll get many links about Python dictionaries, which are a built-in *mapping type* in the language, and not the same thing. So you may need to try synonyms like *GIS, geo, cartography, spatial*, and so on. Popular packages, some of them built atop others in the list, include the following:

PyGIS (https://oreil.ly/3QvCz)
   References for spatial data processing in Python

PySAL (https://pysal.org)
   Python Spatial Analysis Library

Cartopy (https://oreil.ly/YnUow)
 Analyzes and maps geospatial data

Folium (https://oreil.ly/72luj)
 Integrated with JavaScript

Python Client for Google Maps Services (https://oreil.ly/LWfS5)
 API access to Google Maps

Geemap (https://geemap.org)
 Google Earth support

Geoplot (https://oreil.ly/Slfvc)
 Extends Cartopy and Matplotlib

GeoPandas (https://geopandas.org)
 An extension of our friend pandas

ArcGIS and ArcPy (https://oreil.ly/l7M5C)
 Esri's open source interface

Similar to the criteria for plot/graph packages, choices may depend on the following:

- Map types (e.g., choropleth, vector, raster)
- Styling
- Ease of use
- Performance
- Data limits

Like charts and graphs, maps come in many types and can be used for various purposes.

Map Example

I'll use Plotly again for these mapping examples; it's neither too basic nor too complex, and this helps show how to integrate a small web-based map with FastAPI.

Example 17-10 gets the two-letter ISO country codes of our creatures. But it turns out that the function that draws Plotly maps (a *choropleth*, which sounds like a shape-changing cryptid itself) wants to use another *three*-letter ISO country code standard instead. Grrr. So we could redo all the codes in the database and PSV file, but it's easier to run `pip install country_converter` and map one set of country codes to another.

Example 17-10. Map countries with cryptids (edit web/creature.py)

```
# (insert these lines in web/creature.py)

import plotly.express as px
import country_converter as coco

@router.get("/map")
def map():
    creatures = service.get_all()
    iso2_codes = set(creature.country for creature in creatures)
    iso3_codes = coco.convert(names=iso2_codes, to="ISO3")
    fig = px.choropleth(
        locationmode="ISO-3",
        locations=iso3_codes)
    fig_bytes = fig.to_image(format="png")
    return Response(content=fig_bytes, media_type="image/png")
```

Ask your browser to pretty please get **localhost:8000/creature/map**, and with any luck you'll see a map in which cryptid-bearing countries stick out (Figure 17-3).

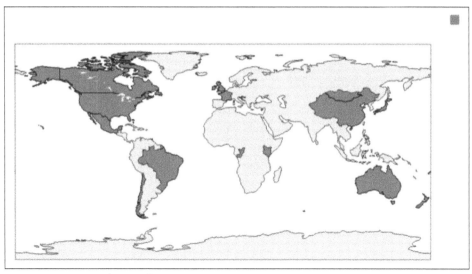

Figure 17-3. Map of cryptid countries

You could expand this map to focus on the US by using the area field, which is a two-character state code if country is US. Use locationmode="USA-states", and assign those area values to the locations parameter of px.choropleth().

Review

Have any cryptids been snuffling around near your house? You found out in this chapter, where various plotting, graphing, and mapping tools poked at a database of worrisome creatures.

## CHAPTER 18

Games

Preview

Games cover a lot of ground, from simple text to multiplayer 3D extravaganzas. This chapter will demonstrate a simple game and how the web endpoint can interact with the user across multiple steps. This process is different from the familiar one-shot request-response web endpoints that you've seen so far.

Python Game Packages

If you really want to get into Python for games, here are some useful tools:

- Text:
  — Adventurelib (*https://adventurelib.readthedocs.io*)
- Graphic:
  — PyGame (*https://www.pygame.org*), primer (*https://realpython.com/pygame-a-primer*)
  — pyglet (*https://pyglet.org*)
  — Python Arcade (*https://api.arcade.academy*)
  — HARFANG (*https://www.harfang3d.com*)
  — Panda3D (*https://docs.panda3d.org*)

But I'm not going to use any of these in this chapter. The example code can get so large and complex that it overshadows the goal of this book: creating websites—APIs and traditional content—with FastAPI, as simply as possible.

Splitting Game Logic

There are so many ways to write a game. Who does what, and who keeps what where—the client or the server? The web is stateless, so each time the client calls the server, the server is a total amnesiac and swears it's never seen this client before. So we need to keep *state* somewhere: data retained across game steps to thread them all together.

We could write a game completely in JavaScript on the client side, and keep all the state there. If you know JavaScript well, that's a good solution, but if you don't (a possibility, because you're reading a Python book), let's give Python something to do too.

At the other extreme, we could write a server-heavy application: generate some distinct id for this particular game on an initial web call, and pass that id with other data to the server in subsequent game steps, and maintain all that changing state in some server-side data store, like a database.

Finally, we could structure the game as a sequence of client-server web endpoint calls, in a so-called single-page application (SPA). Writing an SPA would typically have JavaScript making Ajax calls to a server, and targeting the web responses to refresh parts of the page instead of the whole display. The client JavaScript and HTML do some of the work, and the server handles some of the logic and data.

Game Design

First, what's the game? We'll build a simple Wordle-like game (*https://oreil.ly/PuD-Y*), but using only the names of the creatures from the *cryptid.db* database. This makes it quite a bit easier than Wordle, especially if you cheat and look at Appendix B.

We'll use the final, balanced, design approach above:

1. Let's use vanilla JavaScript in the client instead of well-known JavaScript libraries like React, Angular, or even jQuery.

2. A new FastAPI endpoint, GET /game, initializes the game. It gets a random creature's name from our cryptid database, and returns that, embedded as a hidden value in a Jinja template file of HTML, CSS, and JavaScript.

3. On the client, the newly returned HTML and JavaScript display a Wordle-type interface. A sequence of boxes appears, one for each letter in the hidden creature name.

4. The player types a letter into each box, then submits this guess and the hidden true name to the server. This is in an AJAX call, using the JavaScript fetch() function.

---

5. A second new FastAPI endpoint, POST /game, takes this guess and actual secret name and scores the guess against that name. It returns the guess and score to the client.

6. The client displays the guess and score with appropriate CSS colors in a newly generated table row: green for a letter in the correct place, yellow for a letter in the name but another position, and gray for a letter not occurring in the hidden name. The score is a string of single characters, which are used as CSS class names to display the correct colors for the guess's letters.

7. If all the letters are green, then celebrate accordingly. Otherwise, the client displays a new sequence of text input boxes for the next guess, and repeats the steps 4 and later until the name is guessed or you give up. Most of the cryptid names are not household words, so check Appendix B as needed.

These rules are slightly different from official Wordle, which allows only five-letter dictionary words and a limit of six steps.

Don't get your hopes up. Like most of the examples in this book, the game logic and design are minimal—just enough to get the pieces to work together. You can impart much more style and grace, given a working base.

Web Part One: Game Initialization

We want two new web endpoints. We're using creature names, so we might think of naming endpoints like GET /creature/game and POST /creature/game. But that won't work, because we already have similar endpoints GET /creature/{name} and POST /creature/{name}, and FastAPI will match those first. So let's make a new top-level routing namespace /game, and place both new endpoints under it.

The first endpoint in Example 18-1 initializes the game. It needs to get a random creature name from the database, and return this with all the client code to implement the multistep game logic. For this, we'll use a Jinja template (which you saw in Chapter 16) that contains HTML, CSS, and JavaScript.

Example 18-1. Web game initialization (web/game.py)

```
from pathlib import Path

from fastapi import APIRouter, Body, Request
from fastapi.templating import Jinja2Templates

from service import game as service

router = APIRouter(prefix = "/game")

# Initial game request
```

```
@router.get("")
def game_start(request: Request):
    name = service.get_word()
    top = Path(__file__).resolve().parents[1] # grandparent
    templates = Jinja2Templates(directory=f"{top}/template")
    return templates.TemplateResponse("game.html",
        {"request": request, "word": name})


# Subsequent game requests
@router.post("")
async def game_step(word: str = Body(), guess: str = Body()):
    score = service.get_score(word, guess)
    return score
```

FastAPI requires the game_start() path function to have a request parameter, and to pass it to the template as an argument.

Next, in Example 18-2, hook this /game subrouter into the main module that has been overseeing the /explorer and /creature routes.

Example 18-2. Add /game subroute (web/main.py)

```
from fastapi import FastAPI
from web import creature, explorer, game

app = FastAPI()

app.include_router(explorer.router)
app.include_router(creature.router)
app.include_router(game.router)

if __name__ == "__main__":
    import uvicorn
    uvicorn.run("main:app",
        host="localhost", port=8000, reload=True)
```

Web Part Two: Game Steps

The largest component of the client side template (HTML, CSS, and JavaScript) can be seen in Example 18-3.

Example 18-3. Working Jinja template file (template/game.html)

```
<head>
<style>
html * {
  font-size: 20pt;
  font-family: Courier, sans-serif;
```

```
}
body {
  margin: 0 auto;
  max-width: 700px;
}
input[type=text] {
  width: 30px;
  margin: 1px;
  padding: 0px;
  border: 1px solid black;
}
td, th {
  cell-spacing: 4pt;
  cell-padding: 4pt;
  border: 1px solid black;
}
.H { background-color: #00EE00; } /* hit (green) */
.C { background-color: #EEEE00; } /* close (yellow) */
.M { background-color: #EEEEEE; } /* miss (gray) */
</style>
</head>
<body>
<script>
function show_score(guess, score){
    var table = document.getElementById("guesses");
    var row = table.insertRow(row);
    for (var i = 0; i < guess.length; i++) {
        var cell = row.insertCell(i);
        cell.innerHTML = guess[i];
        cell.classList.add(score[i]);
    }
    var word = document.getElementById("word").value;
    if (guess.toLowerCase() == word.toLowerCase()) {
        document.getElementById("status").innerHTML = "&#x1F600";
    }
}

async function post_guess() {
    var word = document.getElementById("word").value;
    var vals = document.getElementsByName("guess");
    var guess = "";
    for (var i = 0; i < vals.length; i++) {
        guess += vals[i].value;
    }
    var req = new Request("http://localhost:8000/game", {
        method: "POST",
        headers: {"Content-Type": "application/json"},
        body: JSON.stringify({"guess": guess, "word": word})
        }
    )
    fetch(req)
        .then((resp) => resp.json())
```

```
            .then((score) => {
                show_score(guess, score);
                for (var i = 0; i < vals.length; i++) {
                    vals[i].value = "";
                }
            });
}
</script>
<h2>Cryptonamicon</h2>

<table id="guesses">
</table>

<span id="status"></span>

<hr>

<div>
{% for letter in word %}<input type=text name="guess">{% endfor %}
<input type=hidden id="word" value="{{word}}">
<br><br>
<input type=submit onclick="post_guess()">
</div>

</body>
```

Service Part One: Initialization

Example 18-4 shows the Service code to connect the Web layer's game start function to the Data layer's provision of a random creature name.

Example 18-4. Calculate score (service/game.py)

```
import data.game as data

def get_word() -> str:
    return data.get_word()
```

Service Part Two: Scoring

Add the code from Example 18-5 (next) to that of Example 18-4. The score is a string of single characters that indicate whether the guessed letter matched in the correct position, matched in another position, or was a miss. The guess and word are both converted to lowercase to make matching case-insensitive. If the guess is not the same length as the hidden word, an empty string score is returned.

Example 18-5. Calculate score (service/game.py)

```python
from collections import Counter, defaultdict

HIT = "H"
MISS = "M"
CLOSE = "C"  # (letter is in the word, but at another position)

def get_score(actual: str, guess: str) -> str:
    length: int = len(actual)
    if len(guess) != length:
        return ERROR
    actual_counter = Counter(actual) #  {letter: count, ...}
    guess_counter = defaultdict(int)
    result = [MISS] * length
    for pos, letter in enumerate(guess):
        if letter == actual[pos]:
            result[pos] = HIT
            guess_counter[letter] += 1
    for pos, letter in enumerate(guess):
        if result[pos] == HIT:
            continue
        guess_counter[letter] += 1
        if (letter in actual and
            guess_counter[letter] <= actual_counter[letter]):
            result[pos] = CLOSE
    result = ''.join(result)
    return result
```

Test!

Example 18-6 contains some pytest exercises for the service score calculation. It uses pytest's parametrize feature to pass in a sequence of tests, rather than writing a loop inside the test function itself. Remember from Example 18-5 that H is a direct hit, C is close (wrong position), and M is a miss.

Example 18-6. Test score calculation (test/unit/service/test_game.py)

```python
import pytest
from service import game

word = "bigfoot"
guesses = [
    ("bigfoot", "HHHHHHH"),
    ("abcdefg", "MCMMMCC"),
    ("toofgib", "CCCHCCC"),
    ("wronglength", ""),
    ("", ""),
    ]
```

```
@pytest.mark.parametrize("guess,score", guesses)
def test_match(guess, score):
    assert game.get_score(word, guess) == score
```

Run it:

```
$ pytest -q test_game.py
.....                                          [100%]
5 passed in 0.05s
```

Data: Initialization

We only need one function in the new *data/game.py* module, shown in Example 18-7.

Example 18-7. Get random creature name (data/game.py)

```
from .init import curs

def get_word() -> str:
    qry = "select name from creature order by random() limit 1"
    curs.execute(qry)
    row = curs.fetchone()
    if row:
        name = row[0]
    else:
        name = "bigfoot"
    return name
```

Let's Play Cryptonamicon

(Someone, please come up with a better name.)

In your browser, go to `http://localhost:8000/game`. You should see an initial display like this:

Let's type a few letters and submit them as a guess to see what happens:

The letters *b*, *f*, and *g* are yellow (if you're not viewing this in color, you'll have to take my word for it!), meaning they're in the hidden name but in the wrong position:

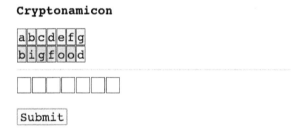

Let's take a stab at the name, but flub the last letter. We see lots of green on the second line. Oh, so close!

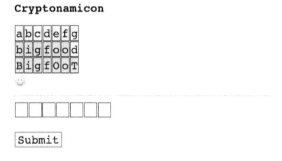

Let's fix that last letter, and just for fun, capitalize some of the letters to ensure that we get case-insensitive matching. Submit that one now, and golly gee:

Cryptonamicon

abcdefg
bigfood
BigfOoT
☺

☐☐☐☐☐☐☐

Submit

Review

We used HTML, JavaScript, CSS, and FastAPI to build a (very!) simple interactive Wordle-style game. This chapter demonstrated how to manage multiple threaded conversations between a web client and server, using JSON and Ajax.

Further Reading

Many great resources are available if you'd like to learn more and fill in the areas that I didn't cover in enough depth or at all. This appendix lists resources for Python, FastAPI, Starlette, and Pydantic.

Python

These are some prominent Python websites:

Python Software Foundation (https://www.python.org)
    The mothership

Real Python Tutorials (https://realpython.com)
    Detailed Python tutorials

Reddit (https://www.reddit.com/r/Python)
    Python subreddit

Stack Overflow (https://stackoverflow.com/questions/tagged/python)
    Questions tagged "Python"

Pycoder's Weekly (https://pycoders.com)
    A weekly email newsletter

Anaconda (https://www.anaconda.com)
    Scientific distribution

These are only some of the Python books that I've found useful while writing this one:

- *Introducing Python*, 2nd edition, by Bill Lubanovic (O'Reilly)
- *Python Distilled* by David Beazley (Pearson Education)
- *Fluent Python* by Luciano Ramalho (O'Reilly)
- *Robust Python* by Patrick Viafore (O'Reilly)
- *Architecture Patterns with Python* by Harry J. W. Percival and Bob Gregory (O'Reilly)

FastAPI

The following are some FastAPI websites:

Home (https://fastapi.tiangolo.com)
    The official site, and the best technical documentation that I've seen

External links and articles (https://fastapi.tiangolo.com/external-links)
    From the official site

FastAPI GitHub (https://github.com/tiangolo/fastapi)
    The FastAPI code repository

Awesome FastAPI (https://github.com/mjhea0/awesome-fastapi)
    A curated list of resources

The Ultimate FastAPI Tutorial (https://oreil.ly/vfvS3)
    A detailed, multipart walk-through

The Blue Book: FastAPI (https://lyz-code.github.io/blue-book/fastapi)
    A detailed overview of FastAPI

Medium (https://medium.com/tag/fastapi)
    Articles tagged "FastAPI"

Using FastAPI to Build Python Web APIs (https://realpython.com/fastapi-python-web-apis)
    Condensed FastAPI docs

Twitter (https://oreil.ly/kHJm_)
    Tweets with @FastAPI or #FastAPI

Gitter (https://oreil.ly/-56rC)
    Help requests and answers

GitHub (https://oreil.ly/NXTU1)
    Repos with FastAPI in their names

Even though FastAPI arrived late in 2018, not many books have popped up yet. Here are some that I've read and learned from:

- *Building Data Science Applications with FastAPI* by François Voron (Packt)
- *Building Python Microservices with FastAPI* by Sherwin John C. Tragura (Packt)
- *Microservice APIs* by José Haro Peralta (Manning)

Starlette

Top links for Starlette include the following:

- Home (*https://www.starlette.io*)
- GitHub (*https://github.com/encode/starlette*)

Pydantic

The main Pydantic links are listed here:

- Home (*https://pydantic.dev*)
- Docs (*https://docs.pydantic.dev*)
- GitHub (*https://github.com/pydantic/pydantic*)

Creatures and Humans

From ghoulies and ghosties
And long-leggetty beasties
And things that go bump in the night
Good Lord deliver us.

    —Verse from a Cornish litany

Imaginary creatures, or *cryptids*, have been reported everywhere. Some animals, once considered imaginary—like the panda, platypus, and black swan—turned out to be real. So we won't speculate. Intrepid explorers are seeking them out. Together, they provide data for the examples in this book.

Creatures

Table B-1 lists the creatures that we'll investigate.

Table B-1. A mini-bestiary

Name	Country	Area	Description	AKA
Abaia	FJ		Lake eel	
Afanc	UK	CYM	Welsh lake monster	
Agropelter	US	ME	Forest twig flinger	
Akkorokamui	JP		Giant Ainu octopus	
Albatwitch	US	PA	Apple-stealing mini Bigfoot	
Alicanto	CL		Gold-eating bird	
Altamata-ha	US	GA	Swamp creature	Altie
Amarok	CA		Inuit wolf spirit	
Auli	CY		Ayia Napa Sea Monster	The Friendly Monster
Azeban	CA		Trickster spirit	The Raccoon
Batsquatch	US	WA	Flying sasquatch	
Beast of Bladenboro	US	NC	Dog bloodsucker	
Beast of Bray Road	US	WI	Wisconsin werewolf	
Beast of Busco	US	IN	Giant turtle	
Beast of Gevaudan	FR		French werewolf	
Beaver Eater	CA		Lodge flipper	Saytoechin
Bigfoot	US		Yeti's Cousin Eddie	Sasquatch
Bukavac	HR		Lake strangler	
Bunyip	AU		Aquatic Aussie	
Cadborosaurus	CA	BC	Sea serpent	Caddie
Champ	US	VT	Lake Champlain lurker	Champy
Chupacabra	MX		Goat bloodsucker	
Dahu	FR		French cousin of Wampahoofus	
Doyarchu	IE		Dog-otter	Irish crocodile
Dragon	*		Wings! Fire!	
Drop Bear	AU		Carnivorous koala	
Dungavenhooter	US		Pounds prey to vapor, then inhales	
Encantado	BR		Frisky river dolphin	
Fouke Monster	US	AR	Stinky bigfoot	Boggy Creek Monster
Glocester Ghoul	US	RI	Rhode Island dragon	
Gloucester Sea Serpent	US	MA	American Nessie	
Igopogo	CA	ON	Canadian Nessie	
Isshii	JP		Lake monster	Issie

Name	Country	Area	Description	AKA
Jackalope	US	*	Antlered rabbit	
Jersey Devil	US	NJ	Snowy roof leaper	
Kodiak Dinosaur	US	AK	Giant ocean saurian	
Kraken	*		Megasquid	
Lizard Man	US	SC	Swamp creature	
LLaammaa	CL		Head of a llama, body of a llama. But not the same llama.	
Loch Ness Monster[a]	UK	SC	Famed loch beastie	Nessie
Lusca	BS		Giant octopus	
Maero	NZ		Giants	
Menehune	US	HI	Hawaiian elves	
Mokele-mbembe	CG		Swamp monster	
Mongolian Death Worm	MN		Arrakis visitor	
Mothman	US	WV	Only cryptid in a Richard Gere movie	
Snarly Yow	US	MD	Hellhound	
Vampire	*		Bloodsucker	
Vlad the Impala	KE		Savannah vampire	
Wendigo	CA		Cannibal bigfoot	
Werewolf	*		Shapeshifter	Loup-garou, Rougarou[b]
Wyvern	UK		Hind-legless dragon	
Wampahoofus	US	VT	Asymmetric mountain dweller	Sidehill Gouger
Yeti	CN		Hirsute Himalayan	Abominable Snowman

[a] I once met Peter MacNab, who took one of the purported photos of Nessie.
[b] French. Or Scooby-Doo: "Ruh-roh! Rougarou!"

Explorers

Our investigative team, from far and wide, is listed in Table B-2.

Table B-2. Humans

Name	Country	Description
Claude Hande	UK	Scarce during full moons
Helena Hande-Basquette	UK	Dame[a] with a claim to fame
Beau Buffette	US	Never removes his pith helmet
O. B. Juan Cannoli	MX	Wise in the ways of the forest
Simon N. Glorfindel	FR	Curly haired, keen-eared woodsman
"Pa" Tuohy	IE	Explorer/expectorator
Radha Tuohy	IN	Mystic earth mother
Noah Weiser	DE	Myopic machete man

[a] In *noblesse*, not *ans*.

Explorer Publications

Here are the imaginary publications of our imaginary explorers:

- *The Secret of Rat Island* by B. Buffette
- *What Was I Thinking?* by O. B. J. Cannoli
- "Spiders Never Sleep," *Journal of Disturbing Results*, by N. Weiser
- "Sehr Böse Spinnen," *Zeitscrift für Vergleichende Kryptozoologie*, by N. Weiser

Other Sources

Cryptid lore has many sources. Some cryptids might be categorized as imaginary creatures, and some may be seen in fuzzy photographs taken at a great distance. My sources included the following:

- "List of Cryptids" Wikipedia page (*https://oreil.ly/7e1ED*)
- "List of Legendary Creatures by Type" Wikipedia page (*https://oreil.ly/1AVfx*)
- The Cryptid Zoo: A Menagerie of Cryptozoology (*http://www.newanimal.org*)
- *The United States of Cryptids* by J. W. Ocker (Quirk Books)
- *In the Wake of the Sea-Serpents* by Bernard Heuvelmans (Hill & Wang)
- *Abominable Snowmen: Legend Come to Life* by Ivan T. Sanderson (Chilton)
- "Every Country Has a Monster" (*https://oreil.ly/yQP7Q*) by Mystery Science Theater
- Bigfoot sightings resources
  - Data on Bigfoot sightings by Tim Renner (*https://oreil.ly/1wMDb*)
  - Bigfoot Sightings Dash App (*https://oreil.ly/b5IKt*)
  - Finding Bigfoot with Dash Part 1 (*https://oreil.ly/0gjCT*), Part 2 (*https://oreil.ly/Lespw*), Part 3 (*https://oreil.ly/aDV8K*)
  - "If It's There, Could It Be a Bear?" (*https://oreil.ly/TlYn7*) by Floe Foxon

Index

F

fake data, 104-109
Faker, 201
FastAPI, 27-47, 87
    advantages of, 27
    asynchronous processing and, 55-56
    automated documentation, 43-46
    automated test forms, 110-112
    defined, 19, 27
    dependencies, 78
    downloading files, 210-211
    Flask versus, 84-86
    Hello? World? application, 28-31
    help resources, 244
    HTTP requests, 32-39
    HTTP responses, 39-43
    installing, 28
    rise of, 22
    uploading files, 207-209
FastAPI Auth Middleware, 163
FastAPI JWT Auth, 163
FastAPI OIDC, 160
FastAPI Repo Issues page, 160
FastAPI Resource Server, 160
FastAPI Users, 163
fastapi-auth0, 163
fastapi-authz, 163
fastapi-jwt, 163
FastAPI-key-auth, 163
FastAPI-Login, 163
fastapi-opa, 163
fastapi-sso, 163
fastapi-third-party-auth, 160
FastAPI-User-Auth, 163
fastapi_auth2, 163
Fastest Fish, 208
Fielding, Roy, 5
file and directory layout
    Service layer, 116
    Web layer, 97-98
File(), 208
FileResponse, 210
files, 207-213
    downloading, 87, 210-211
    multipart support, 207
    performance and, 189
    static files, 211-213
    uploading, 87, 207-209
Flask, 22, 83-86, 87

    body, 85
    headers, 86
    query parameters, 85
    URL paths, 84
Folium, 230
forms, 215-217
    GET forms, 215-216
    POST forms, 217
frontend, 4
full (end-to-end; contract) tests
    automated, 180-182
    Data layer, 131-140
    defined, 166
function return type hints, 63
functools, 189

G

games, 233-242
    example game, 234-242
    game packages, 233
    splitting logic, 234-242
Geemap, 230
generators, 52-53
GeoPandas, 230
Geoplot, 230
gevent, 51
Git, 19
global authentication, 145-148
Grafana, 191
GraphQL, 8
Grasshopper, 183
green threads, 51
greenlet, 51
gRPC, 4
Gunicorn, 186

H

HARFANG, 233
histograms, 228-229
Holovaty, Adrian, 22
HTML, 5
HTML forms, 87
HTTP, 5
HTTP requests, 6, 32-39
    body, 36-37
    headers, 37-38
    multiple request data, 38
    query parameters, 34-36
    URL paths, 33-34

About the Author

Bill Lubanovic has been a developer for over 40 years, specializing in Linux, the web, and Python. He coauthored the O'Reilly book *Linux System Administration* and wrote both editions of *Introducing Python*. He discovered FastAPI a few years ago and, with his team, used it to rewrite a large biomedical research API. The experience was so positive that they've adopted FastAPI for all new projects. Bill lives with his family and cats in the Sangre de Sasquatch mountains of Minnesota.

Colophon

The animal on the cover of *FastAPI* is a spiny-tailed iguana (of the genus *Ctenosaura*). The name Ctenosaura comes from two Greek words: ctenos (meaning comb, for the comblike spine on their back and tail) and saura (lizard). There are 15 recognized types of spiny-tailed iguana, including five-keeled, black-chested, Motagua, Oaxaca, Roatán, and Útila.

Spiny-tailed iguanas can range in size from 4.9 to 39 inches long. Each species has a different color that can change based on their body temperature, mood, health, and habitat temperature. Some of the colors include brown, black, gray, pink, green, and yellow. In general, spiny-tailed iguanas are omnivores that eat a variety of fruits, flowers, foliage, and small animals.

While iguanas can be found in a variety of habitats, spiny-tailed iguanas are native to Mexico and Central America. They can be found in tropical and subtropical dry forests, scrubland, and occasionally in human-altered habitats and urban areas. Some species, like Roatán (only found on the Honduran Bay island of Roatán), Útila (only found on Útila, a Bay Island archipelago off of the Caribbean coast of Honduras, in swamps and mangrove ecosystems), and Motagua (found only in Guatemala) are endemic to very specific areas.

Several species of spiny-tailed iguanas are listed as endangered or critically endangered. A few are also known to be invasive species in the United States (western and black spiny-tailed iguanas). They face a number of threats, including habitat loss due to agriculture and cattle grazing, illegal pet trade and poaching, habitat fragmentation, introduced predators, and fear-based killing. Many of the animals on O'Reilly covers are endangered; all of them are important to the world.

The cover illustration is by Karen Montgomery, based on an antique engraving from *Museum of Animated Nature*. The cover fonts are Gilroy Semibold and Guardian Sans. The text font is Adobe Minion Pro; the heading font is Adobe Myriad Condensed; and the code font is Dalton Maag's Ubuntu Mono.

9 781098 135508